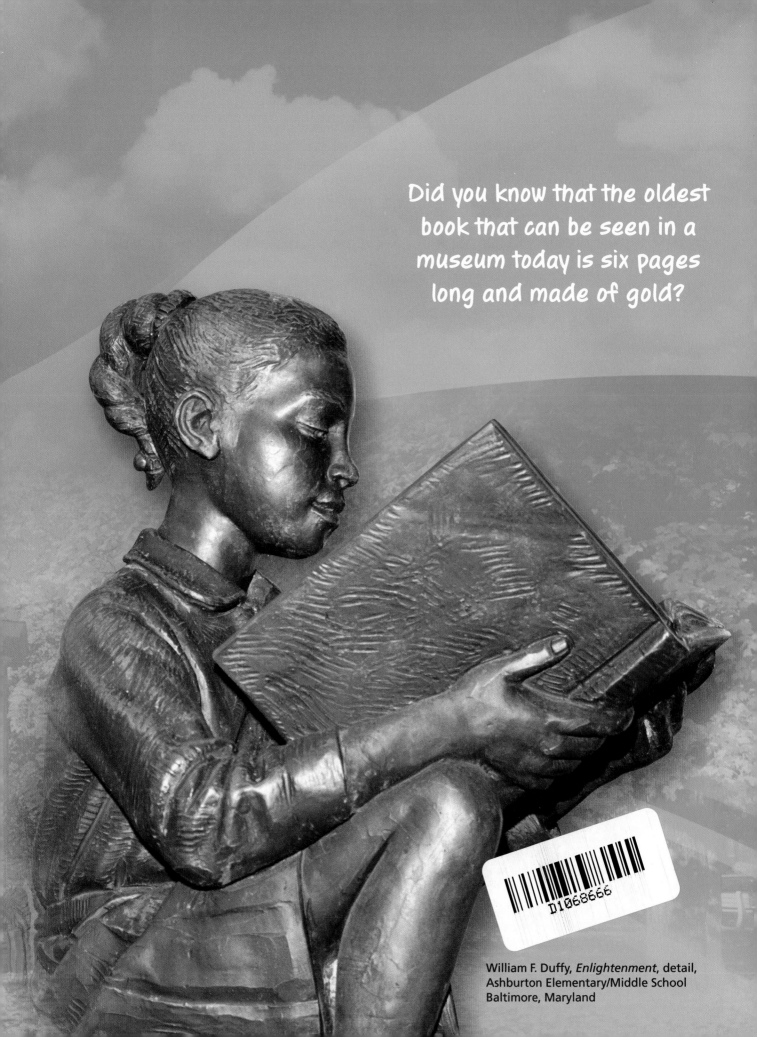

Did you know that the oldest book that can be seen in a museum today is six pages long and made of gold?

William F. Duffy, *Enlightenment*, detail, Ashburton Elementary/Middle School Baltimore, Maryland

INDIANA SOCIAL Studies

People We Know

HOUGHTON MIFFLIN HARCOURT
School Publishers

INDIANA SOCIAL Studies

People We Know

Series Authors

Dr. Michael J. Berson
Professor
Social Science Education
University of South Florida
Tampa, Florida

Dr. Tyrone C. Howard
Associate Professor
UCLA Graduate School of Education & Information Studies
University of California at Los Angeles
Los Angeles, California

Dr. Cinthia Salinas
Assistant Professor
Department of Curriculum and Instruction
College of Education
The University of Texas at Austin
Austin, Texas

Series Consultants

Dr. Marsha Alibrandi
Assistant Professor of Social Studies
Curriculum and Instruction Department
North Carolina State University
Raleigh, North Carolina

Dr. Patricia G. Avery
Professor
College of Education and Human Development
University of Minnesota
Minneapolis/St. Paul, Minnesota

Dr. Linda Bennett
Associate Professor
College of Education
University of Missouri–Columbia
Columbia, Missouri

Dr. Walter C. Fleming
Department Head and Professor
Native American Studies
Montana State University
Bozeman, Montana

Dr. S. G. Grant
Associate Professor
University at Buffalo
Buffalo, New York

C. C. Herbison
Lecturer
African and African-American Studies
University of Kansas
Lawrence, Kansas

Dr. Eric Johnson
Assistant Professor
Director, Urban Education Program
School of Education
Drake University
Des Moines, Iowa

Dr. Bruce E. Larson
Professor
Social Studies Education
Secondary Education
Woodring College of Education
Western Washington University
Bellingham, Washington

Dr. Merry M. Merryfield
Professor
Social Studies and Global Education
College of Education
The Ohio State University
Columbus, Ohio

Dr. Peter Rees
Associate Professor
Department of Geography
University of Delaware
Wilmington, Delaware

Dr. Phillip J. VanFossen
James F. Ackerman Professor of Social Studies Education
Associate Director, Purdue Center for Economic Education
Purdue University
West Lafayette, Indiana

Dr. Myra Zarnowski
Professor
Elementary and Early Childhood Education
Queens College
The City University of New York
Flushing, New York

Classroom Reviewers and Contributors

Jenny Abell
Teacher
Crooked Creek Elementary
Indianapolis, Indiana

Marsha Blevins
Teacher
Earlywine Elementary School
Oklahoma City, Oklahoma

Barbara Clark
Teacher
Southwind Elementary School
Memphis, Tennessee

Connie Deiwert
Teacher
Maple Grove Elementary
Bargersville, Indiana

Kelly Fusco
Teacher
Mackeben Elementary School
Algonquin, Illinois

Dr. Chrystal S. Johnson
Assistant Professor
Social Studies Education
Department of Curriculum and Instruction
Purdue University
West Lafayette, Indiana

Amy Kreuzer
Teacher
Fouse Elementary School
Westerville, Ohio

Kim Louis
Teacher
Lakeland Elementary School
Lakeland, Tennessee

Regina Nargessi
Teacher
Walton-Verona Elementary School
Verona, Kentucky

Cindy Royalty
Teacher
E. O. Muncie Elementary
Madison, Indiana

ISBN-13: 978-0-15-377042-5
ISBN-10: 0-15-377042-2

1 2 3 4 5 6 7 8 9 10 048 17 16 15 14 13 12 11 10 09 08

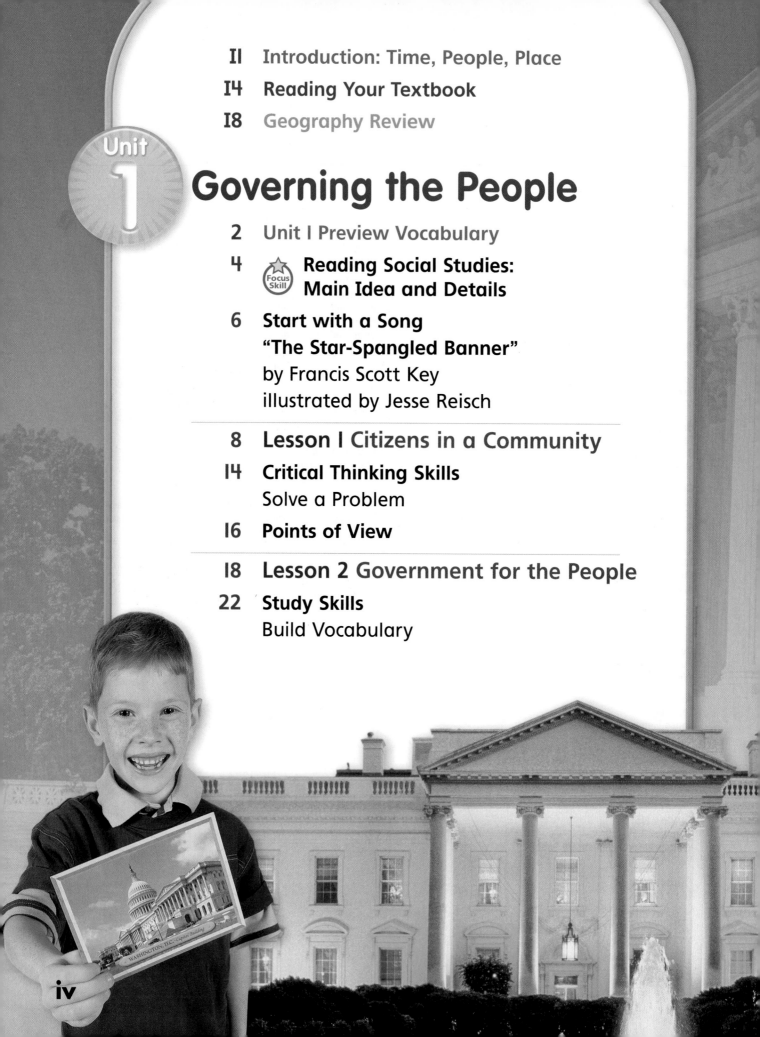

Unit 1

Governing the People

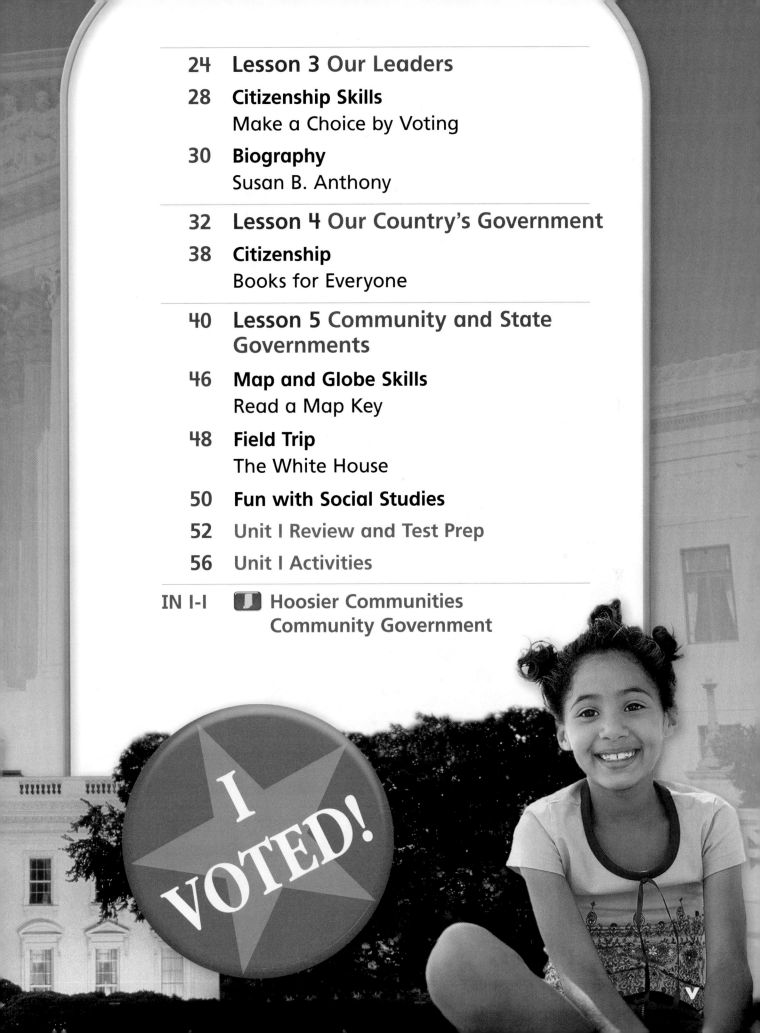

v

Unit 2

The World Around Us

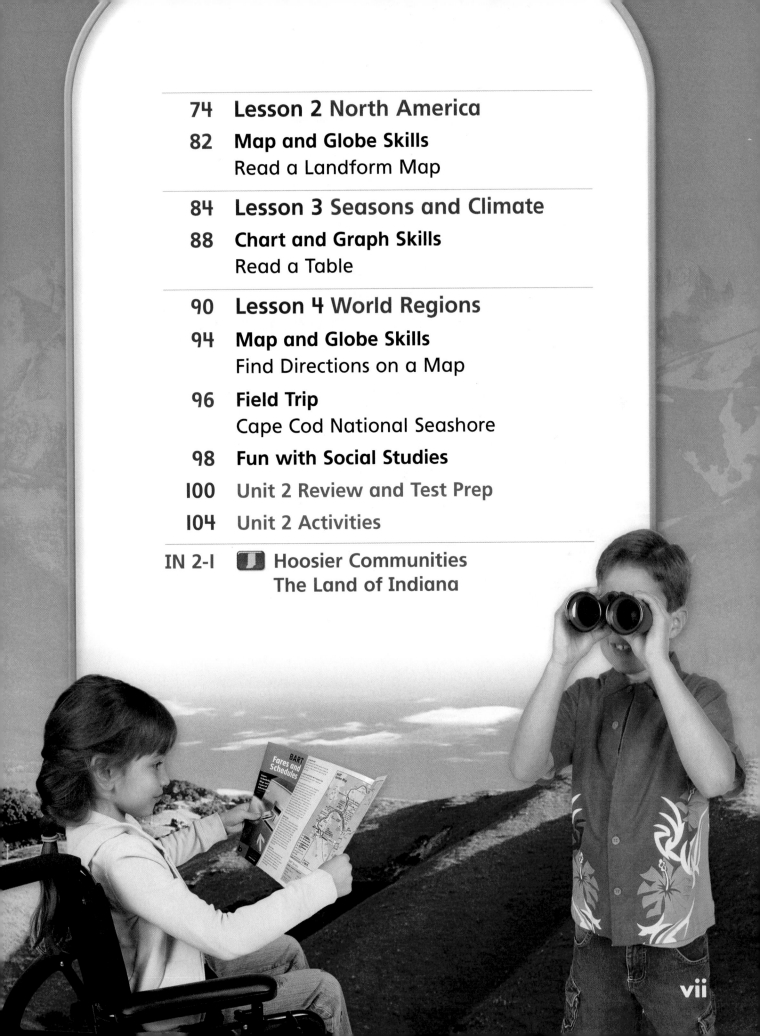

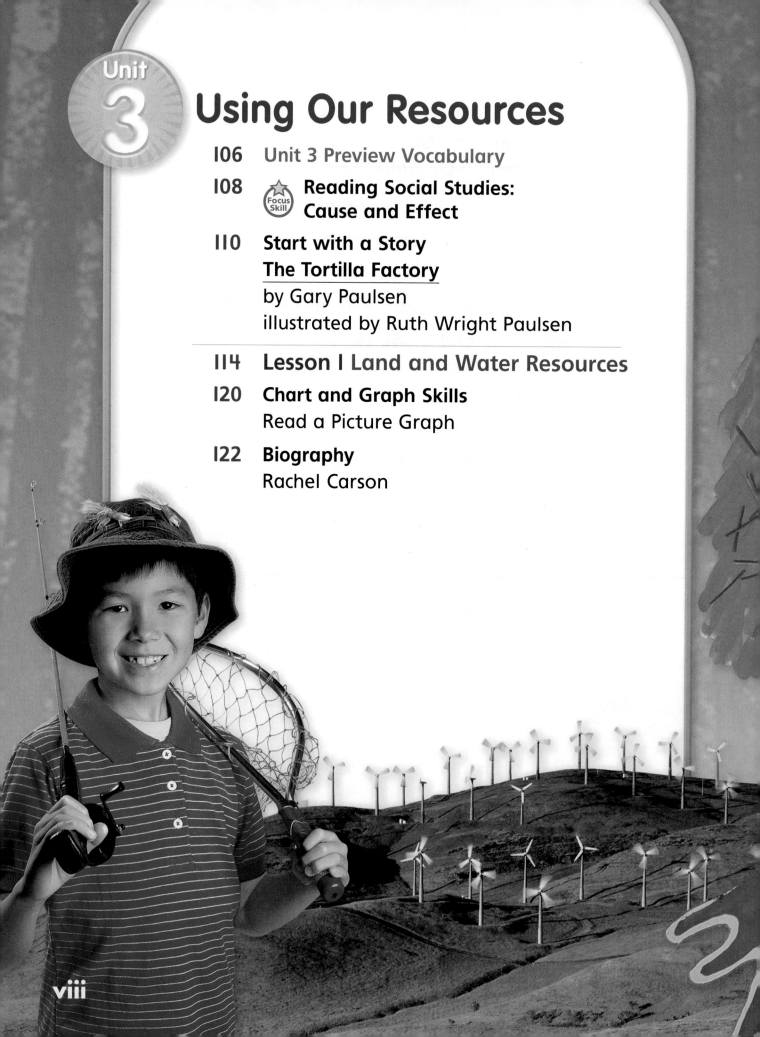

Unit 3

Using Our Resources

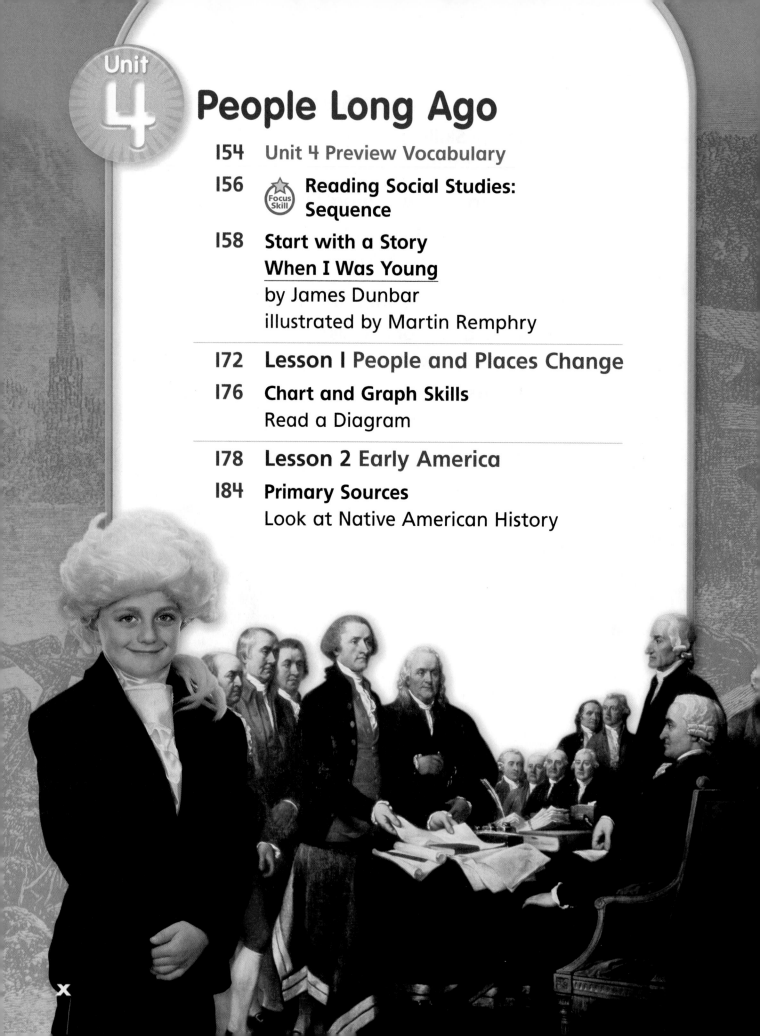

Unit 4

People Long Ago

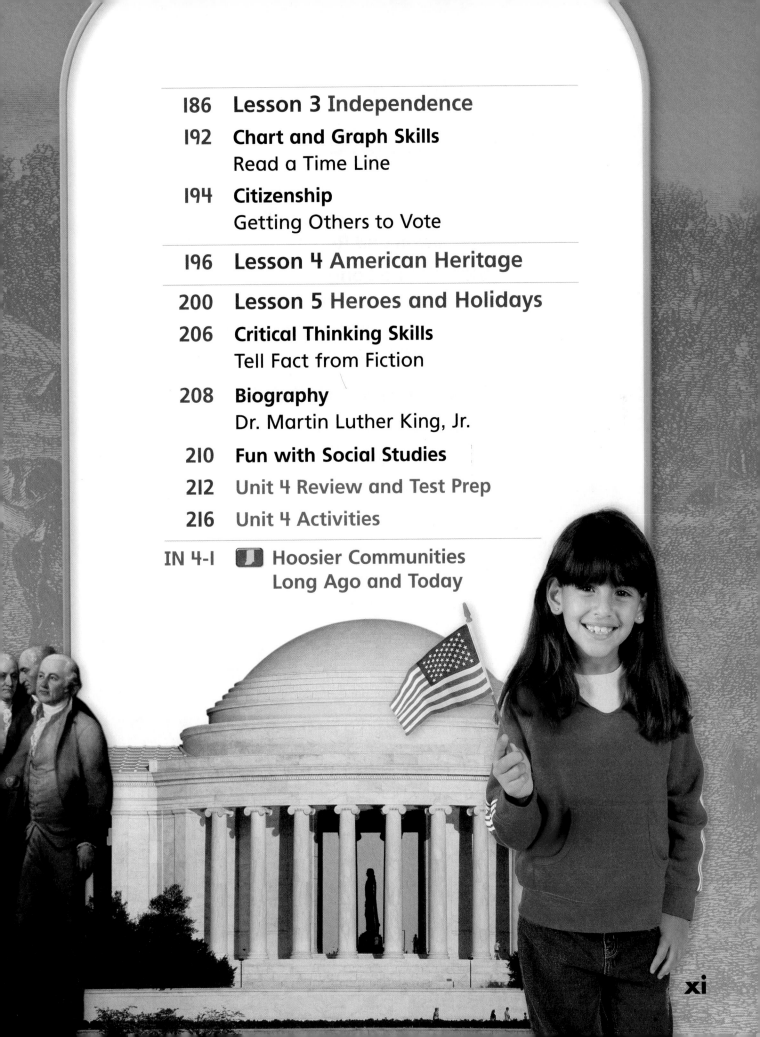

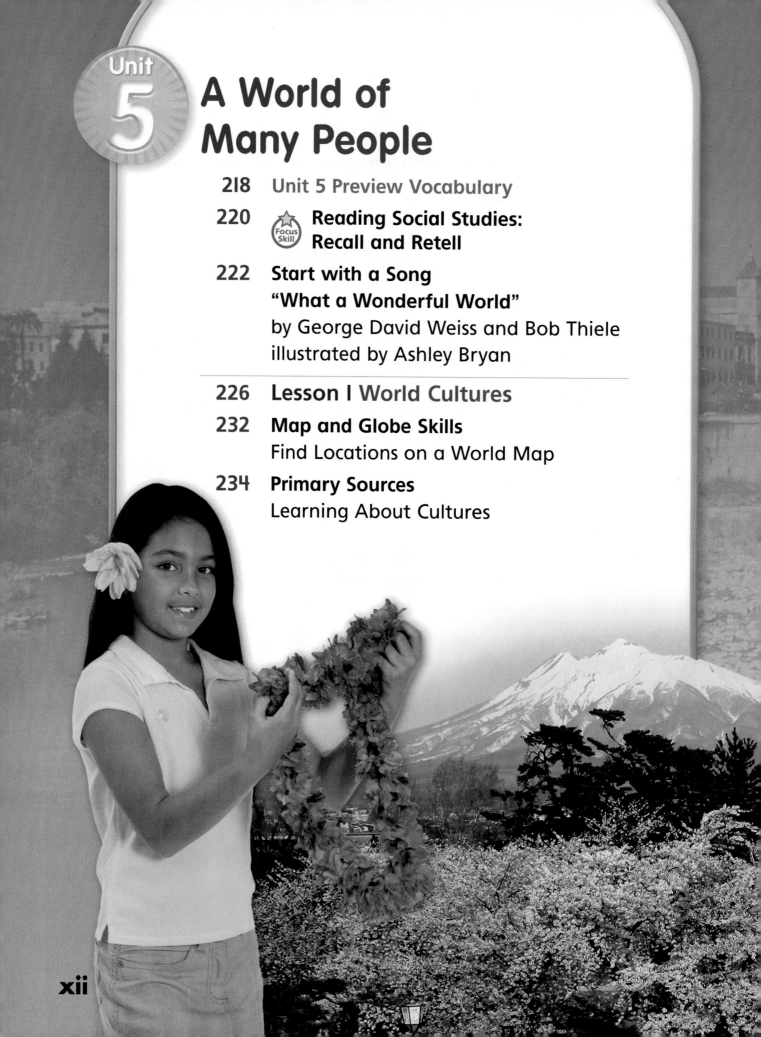

Unit 5

A World of Many People

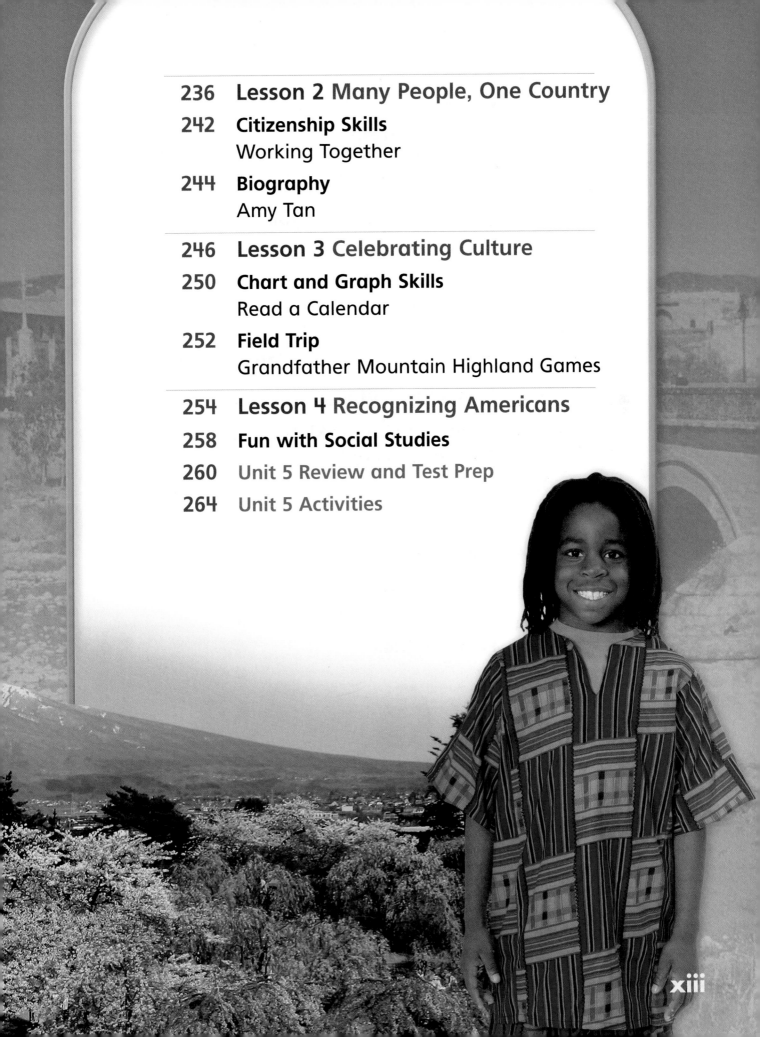

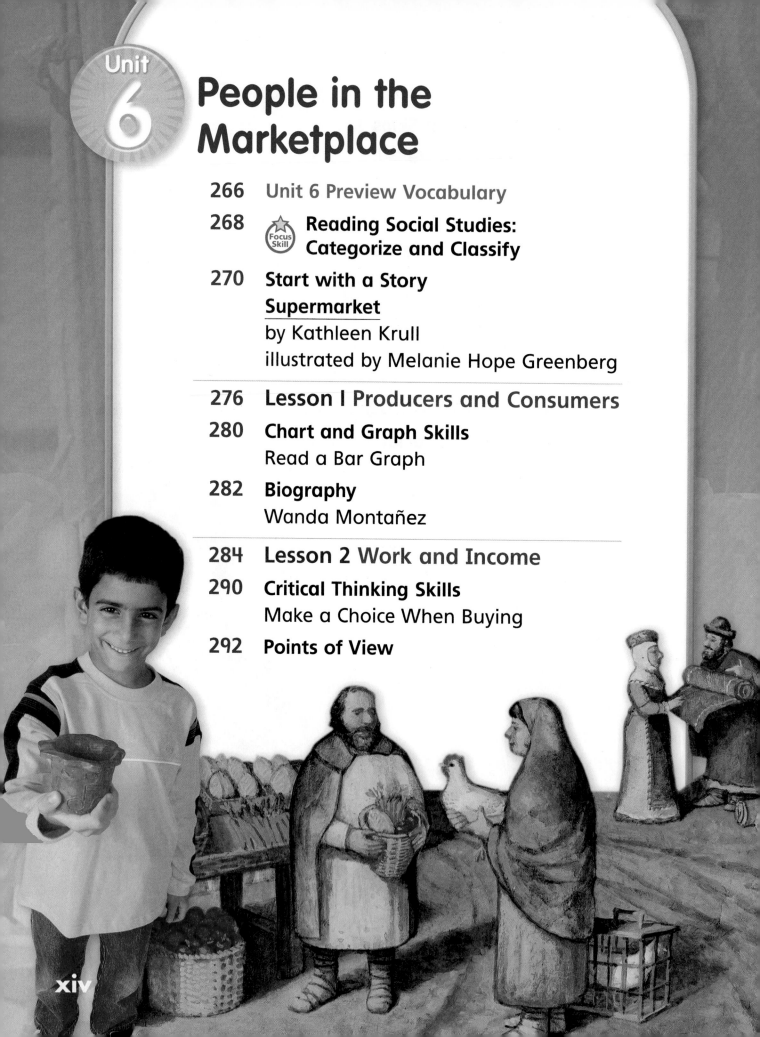

Unit 6

People in the Marketplace

Hair Salon

Shoe Store

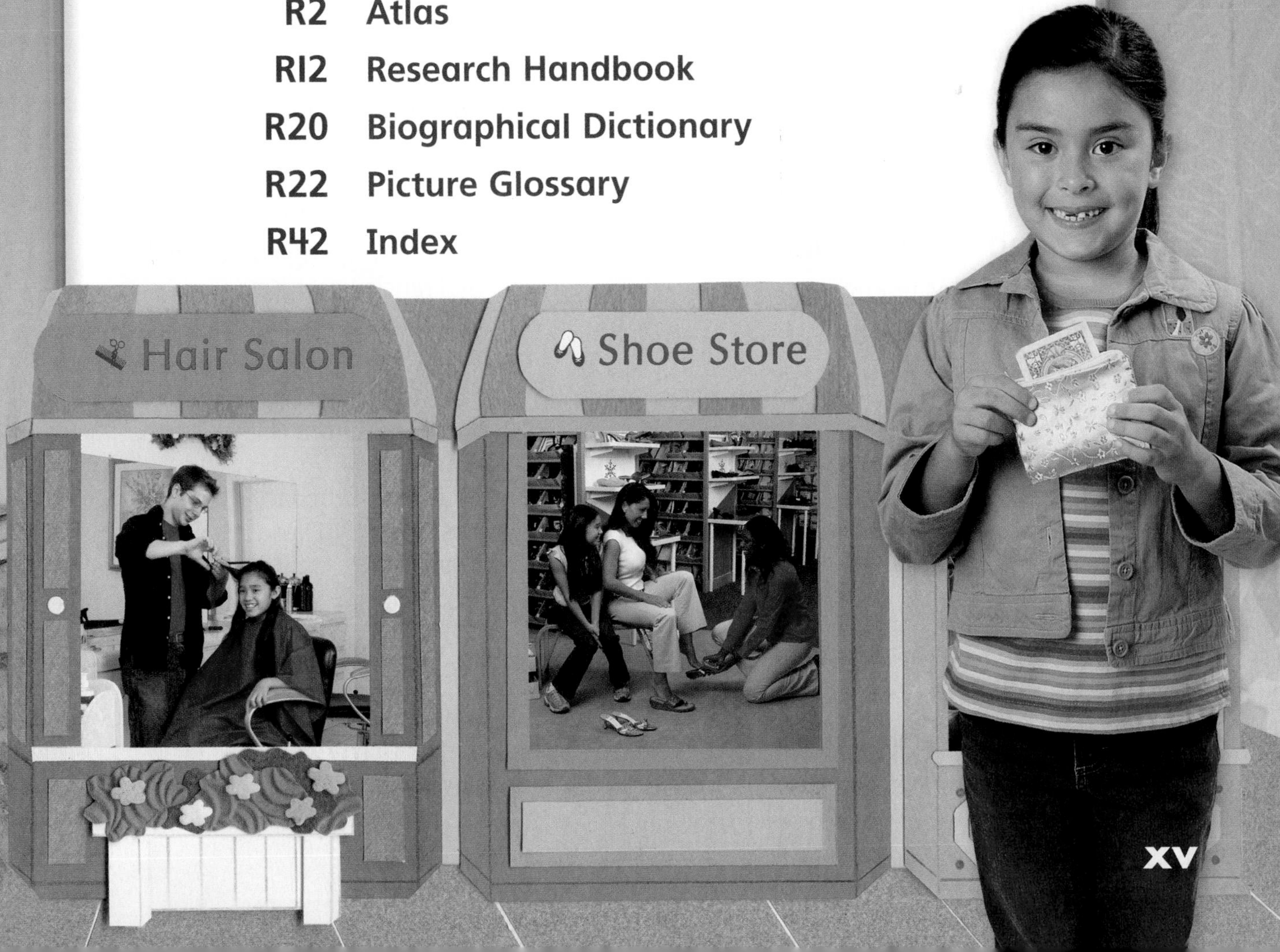

Features

Maps

Time Line

Illustrations

The Story Well Told

"I wanted children now to understand more about the beginnings of things . . . what it is that made America as they know it."

Laura Ingalls Wilder in *Laura Ingalls Wilder: A Biography*

by W. Anderson

Do you ever wonder about people who lived in a different time or place? This year you will be learning about how families have changed over **time**. You will meet special **people** who we remember for the important work they have done. Also, you will visit **places** near and far. You will see where people live and how they use the land around them.

People We Know

The Story Is About Time, People, and Place

You can learn how people lived long ago by reading the story of a family's past.

Important people teach us how to behave.

We get most of our resources from the land.

Reading Your Textbook

GETTING STARTED

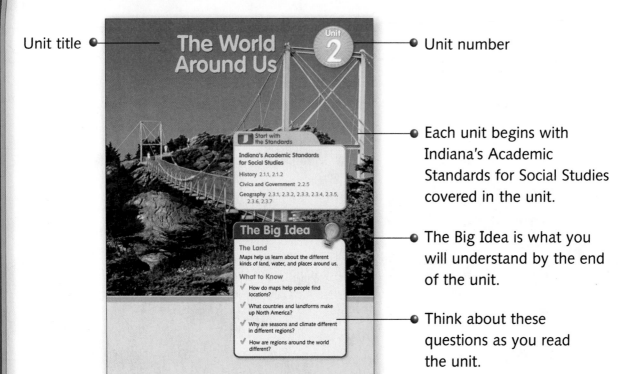

Unit title

Unit number

Each unit begins with Indiana's Academic Standards for Social Studies covered in the unit.

The Big Idea is what you will understand by the end of the unit.

Think about these questions as you read the unit.

PREVIEW VOCABULARY

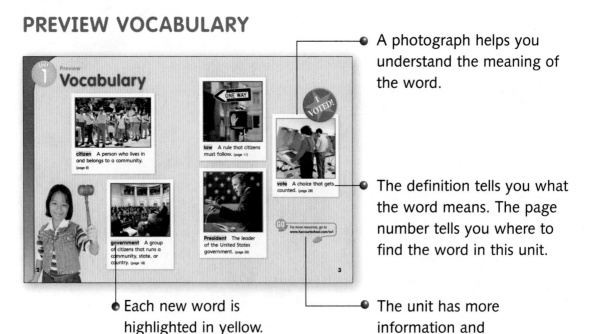

A photograph helps you understand the meaning of the word.

The definition tells you what the word means. The page number tells you where to find the word in this unit.

Each new word is highlighted in yellow.

The unit has more information and activities on the website.

READING SOCIAL STUDIES

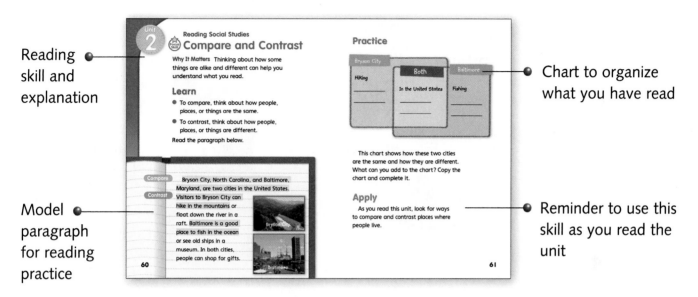

Reading skill and explanation

Model paragraph for reading practice

Chart to organize what you have read

Reminder to use this skill as you read the unit

START WITH LITERATURE

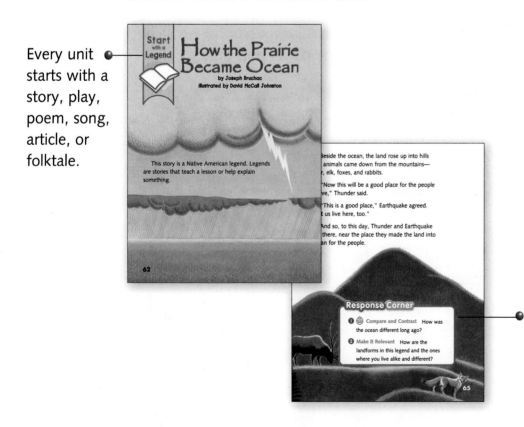

Every unit starts with a story, play, poem, song, article, or folktale.

Questions to practice the unit reading skill and to talk about personal experiences

READING A LESSON

Lesson number

Guiding question

New words to learn

Reminder to use your reading skill

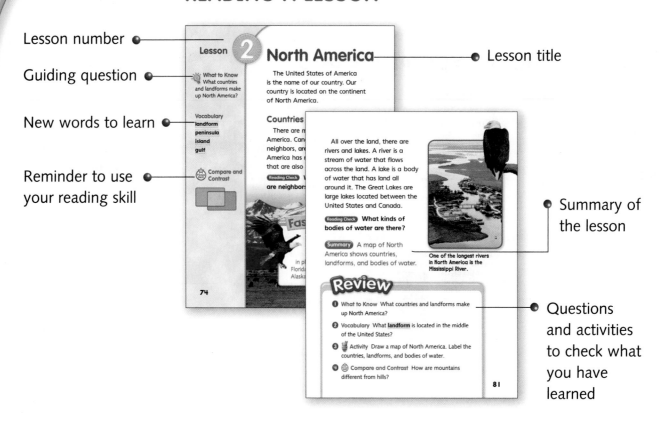

Lesson title

Summary of the lesson

Questions and activities to check what you have learned

PRACTICING SKILLS

Skill lessons help you build your map and globe, chart and graph, study, critical thinking, and citizenship skills.

Skill category

Skill lesson title

Why the skill is important

Steps to learn the skill

Skill practice questions

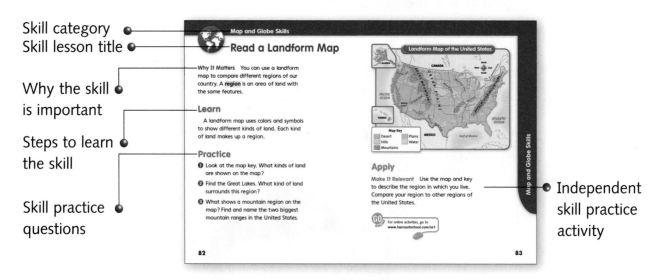

Independent skill practice activity

SPECIAL FEATURES

Name of the biography

Discussion of the person's character

Website for more information and other biographies

Important dates in the person's life

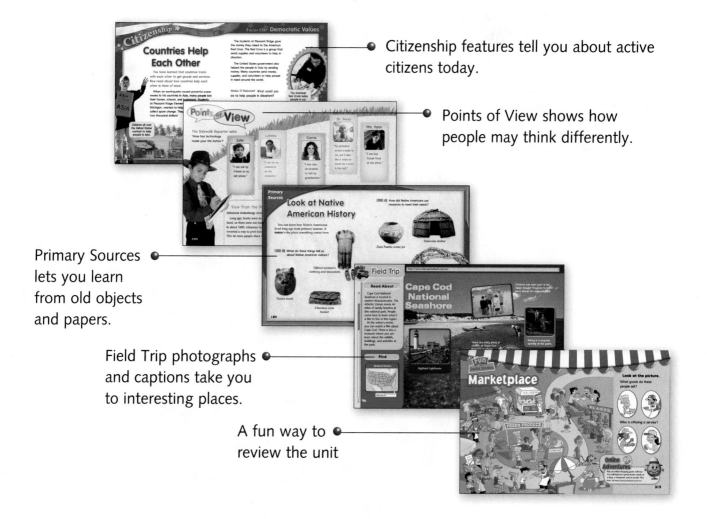

Citizenship features tell you about active citizens today.

Points of View shows how people may think differently.

Primary Sources lets you learn from old objects and papers.

Field Trip photographs and captions take you to interesting places.

A fun way to review the unit

Go to the Reference section in the back of this book to see other special features.

The Five Themes of Geography

The story of people is also the story of where they live. When scientists talk about Earth, they think about five themes or main ideas.

Location

Everything on Earth has its own place.

Place

Every place has features that make it different from other places.

GEOGRAPHY

Human-Environment Interactions

People can change their surroundings.

Movement

Each day, people around the world trade goods and ideas.

THEMES

Regions

Areas of Earth share features that make them different from other areas.

Looking at Earth

The shape of Earth is shown best by a globe. A **globe** is a model of our planet.

On a map of the world you can see all the land and water at once. A **map** is a flat drawing that shows where places are.

Much of the world is covered by large areas of water called oceans.

A continent is one of seven main land areas on Earth.

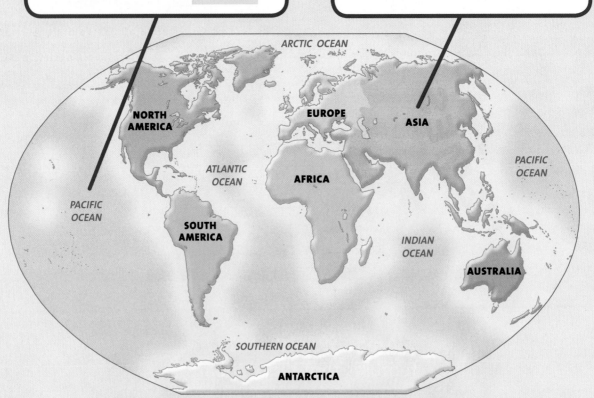

ARCTIC OCEAN

NORTH AMERICA

EUROPE

ASIA

ATLANTIC OCEAN

AFRICA

PACIFIC OCEAN

PACIFIC OCEAN

SOUTH AMERICA

INDIAN OCEAN

AUSTRALIA

SOUTHERN OCEAN

ANTARCTICA

MAP SKILL Name the seven continents and five oceans you see on the map.

Your Address

You live on the continent of North America in a **country** called the United States. Your address names the **city** and **state** in which you live.

North America
continent

United States
country

Indiana
state
city
Indianapolis

Mari Tyler
123 Pine Street
Indianapolis, IN 46205

What is your address?

View from Above

Does your neighborhood have a school, a grocery store, a library, a fire station, a park, and a bank? These are places that people share in a neighborhood. You can learn about a neighborhood by looking at a photograph.

How does a photograph taken from above help you study a neighborhood?

You can also learn about a neighborhood by looking at a map. Mapmakers draw symbols to help you find places on the map. A **map symbol** is a small picture or shape that stands for a real thing. The **map title** tells you what the map shows.

How is this map like the photograph? How is it different?

Neighborhood Map

desert a large, dry area of land

forest a large area of trees

gulf a large body of ocean water that is partly surrounded by land

hill land that rises above the land around it

island a landform with water all around it

lake a body of water with land on all sides

mountain highest kind of land

ocean a body of salt water that covers a large area

peninsula a landform that is surrounded on only three sides by water

plain flat land

river a large stream of water that flows across the land

valley low land between hills or mountains

Governing
the People

Start with the Standards

Indiana's Academic Standards
for Social Studies

History 2.1.3, 2.1.4

Civics and Government 2.2.1, 2.2.2, 2.2.3,
2.2.4, 2.2.5, 2.2.6, 2.2.7

Geography 2.3.2, 2.3.3, 2.3.4, 2.3.5, 2.3.7

The Big Idea

Government

A government makes laws to help people
be safe and get along.

What to Know

✔ How can citizens be responsible in their
community?

✔ How does government help people?

✔ Why do we need leaders?

✔ How does our country's government
work?

✔ What are the jobs of our community
and state governments?

Community Government

Did You Know?

Lake County was named for its location on Lake Michigan.

Communities in Indiana have their own governments. Each government makes laws for its community. It also hires police officers and firefighters to keep people safe.

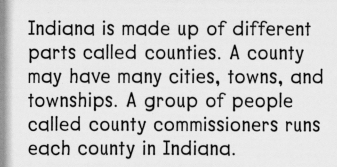

Indiana is made up of different parts called counties. A county may have many cities, towns, and townships. A group of people called county commissioners runs each county in Indiana.

Small towns in Indiana are led by a town board. Each town board has between three and seven members. A trustee leads each town board.

Most large cities in Indiana are run by a city council and a mayor. The city council makes laws. The mayor makes sure that the laws are followed.

Indiana TEST PREP

1. What does a mayor do?
   A makes laws for the city
   B makes sure that laws are followed
   C makes laws for small towns
   D makes sure laws are fair

2. Who leads most small towns in Indiana?
   A a mayor and a commissioner
   B a city council and a mayor
   C a town board
   D county commissioners

3. **Writing** What kinds of leaders run local governments in Indiana?

Governing the People

Talk About

Government

"The Supreme Court makes sure laws are fair."

"American citizens are proud of their country."

"People visit Washington, D.C., to see many government buildings."

Vocabulary

citizen   A person who lives in and belongs to a community.

(page 8)

government   A group of citizens that runs a community, state, or country. (page 18)

law A rule that citizens must follow. (page 11)

vote A choice that gets counted. (page 28)

President The leader of the United States government. (page 26)

GO ONLINE For more resources, go to www.harcourtschool.com/ss1

Reading Social Studies

Focus Skill

Main Idea and Details

Why It Matters When you read for information, look for the main ideas and important details.

Learn

Good paragraphs have a main idea and details.

- The main idea is the most important part of what you are reading.

- The details explain the main idea.

Read the paragraph below.

Main Idea Our town is planning a new community center.
Detail The center will be big enough for special events. It will have classes and fun activities for adults. It will also have after-school programs for children. Our new community center will have something for everyone!

Practice

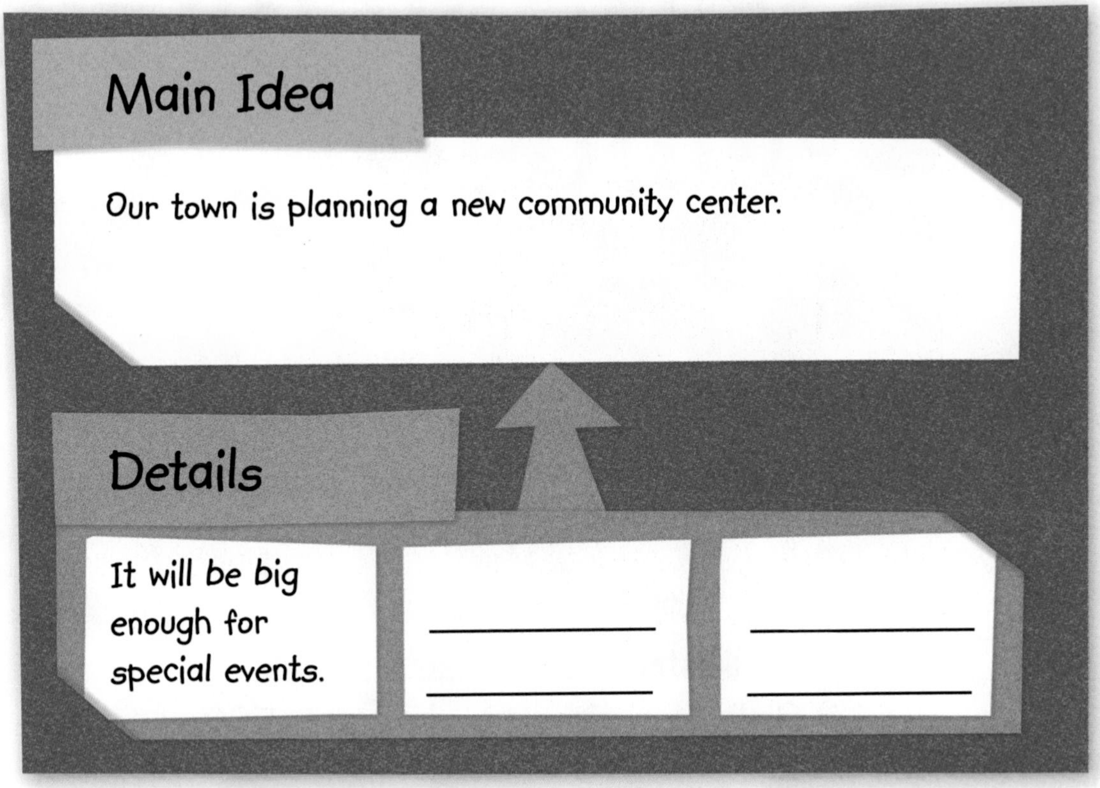

Main Idea

Our town is planning a new community center.

Details

| It will be big enough for special events. | _____ _____ | _____ _____ |

This chart shows the main idea and one detail from what you just read. Copy the chart and complete it.

Apply

As you read this unit, look for the main ideas and details about what governments do.

Start with a Song

The Star-Spangled Banner

by Francis Scott Key
illustrated by Jesse Reisch

Oh, say, can you see,
by the dawn's early light,
What so proudly we hailed
at the twilight's last gleaming,

Whose broad stripes and bright stars,
through the perilous fight,
O'er the ramparts we watched, were so
gallantly streaming?

And the rockets' red glare,
the bombs bursting in air,
Gave proof through the night
that our flag was still there.

Oh, say, does that star-spangled
banner yet wave,
O'er the land of the free
and the home of the brave?

Response Corner

1. ⭐ **Focus Skill** **Main Ideas and Details** What does this song tell about the United States flag?

2. **Make It Relevant** Where have you heard this song sung in your community?

What to Know
How can citizens be responsible in their community?

Vocabulary

community

citizen

right

responsibility

law

consequence

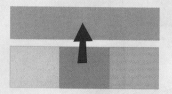
Main Idea and Details

Citizens in a Community

Every day, you work and play with others. People who work and play together live in a **community**. Your family and school are part of a community. The people who belong to a community are its **citizens**.

St. Louis, Missouri

Citizens Have Rights

What does it mean to be a citizen? In the United States, it means having rights. A **right** is a kind of freedom.

Americans have important rights. We can live and work where we want. We can follow our religious beliefs and share our ideas.

Reading Check (Focus Skill) **Main Idea and Details**

What is a community?

Citizens Have Responsibilities

Every person plays many roles, or parts, in a community. Each role has responsibilities. A **responsibility** is something you should take care of or do. A student is responsible for learning. A family member is responsible for helping. A citizen is responsible for taking care of the community and respecting people's rights.

Reading Check **What is your responsibility as a student?**

10

Rules and Laws

All communities have rules. Some rules are called laws. A **law** is a rule that citizens must follow. Rules and laws help us stay safe and protect our rights. They help us learn, work, and play together. Rules and laws also help us solve problems fairly.

Street signs show laws everyone must follow.

It is our responsibility to follow rules and laws so that no one is hurt or treated unfairly. People who break rules must face consequences. A **consequence** is something that happens because of what a person does or does not do.

If a child breaks a rule at school, the consequence might be not being allowed to do something fun. People who break laws may have to do work for the community or pay money. People who break the most important laws must go to jail.

PARKING VIOLATION

☐ Letting the meter run out

☑ Blocking a fire hydrant

☐ Double-parking

Fine..............$65

Reading Check **Why is it important to follow rules and laws?**

Summary Citizens in a community have rights and responsibilities. They must follow rules and laws to be safe and get along.

Review

① **What to Know** How can citizens be responsible in their community?

② **Vocabulary** What can be a **consequence** of not following a rule or a law?

③ ✏ **Write** Think of a rule in your classroom or school. Explain why it is important to follow the rule.

④ **Main Idea and Details** What is a right you have as a citizen?

Solve a Problem

Why It Matters Citizens in communities work together to solve problems. A **problem** is something that makes things difficult.

Learn

A **solution** is a way to solve a problem. Sometimes there is more than one solution to a problem. Follow these steps.

❶ Name the problem.

❷ Gather information.

❸ Think about different solutions.

❹ Think about the consequences of each solution.

❺ Try a solution.

❻ Think about how well the solution worked.

Practice

Look at the picture. Name the problem that needs to be solved. Make a list of possible solutions.

Apply

Choose the solution you think is best. Write a paragraph telling what the problem is and why you think the solution will work.

Points of View

The Sidewalk Reporter asks:

"What do you do to get along with your neighbors?"

Amanda

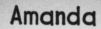

"I clean up after my dog."

Mr. Kim

"I keep my home and yard neat."

View from the Past

Anyokah: Getting Along

In 1817, six-year-old Anyokah began working with her father, Sequoyah, to help the people of her community get along. By 1821, they had created an alphabet for the Cherokee people.

16

Josh

"I drive slowly and watch for people."

Mrs. Avila

"I work on the city council."

Elena

"I don't litter. I use trash cans in the park."

It's Your Turn

- Do you do any of the things that these citizens do? If so, which ones?
- What do you do to get along with your neighbors? What laws do you obey?

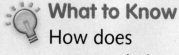
💡 **What to Know**
How does
government help
people?

Vocabulary
government
judge
government
    service
tax

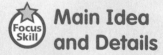 **Main Idea
and Details**

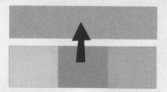

Government for the People

In a community, people form groups to get what they need and want. Many different groups work together to help each other.

We Need Government

All communities have a **government**, or a group of citizens that runs the community. The government makes laws to keep its citizens safe. It makes sure that people get along.

When people do not agree, a court may decide how everyone can be treated fairly. Courts are a part of government.

The person in charge of a court is a **judge**. A judge makes sure that the court protects the rights of all citizens.

Judge Orlando Hudson, Jr., of North Carolina

 Main Idea and Details

What does a government do?

A school board, teachers, and parents work together to help schools.

Government Services

A **government service** is something that the government of a community provides for all the citizens. Government services include roads, schools, and parks. Police and fire departments are other government services. These services help to keep citizens safe.

Government services cost money. Citizens pay for them with taxes. A **tax** is money people pay to the government. The government makes choices about how the tax money will be spent.

Reading Check How do government services make a community better?

Summary A government is a group of people that runs a community. It protects citizens and provides services they need.

1. **What to Know** How does government help people?

2. **Vocabulary** How does a **judge** help a community?

3. ✏️ **Write** Write a thank-you note for a government service. Tell how the service helps you.

4. (Focus Skill) **Main Idea and Details** What do taxes pay for?

Build Vocabulary

Why It Matters   Learning new words helps you understand what you read. It also helps you use the right words to talk about your ideas.

Learn

Making a word web is one way to show how words are connected. The main idea goes in the middle circle.

Practice

Copy the word web shown on the next page.

❶ Add more words about a community.

❷ What do the words tell you about a community?

22

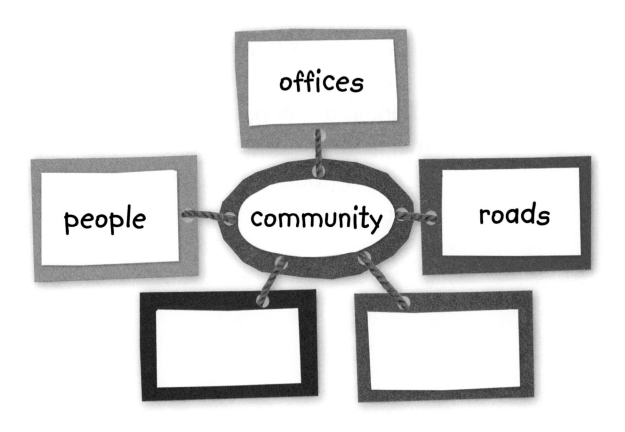

Apply

Make a word web for <u>government</u>. As you read more about government, add words to your web.

Our Leaders

Vocabulary
election
mayor
governor
President

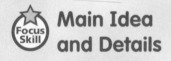

Focus Skill **Main Idea and Details**

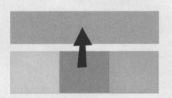

A leader is a person who helps others get a job done. When people work in a group, a good leader helps them decide how they can reach a goal. A good leader also treats others with respect.

Choosing Leaders

In the United States, citizens choose leaders to run the government. Government leaders work to keep people safe and to keep order.

Citizens choose many of their government leaders at events called **elections**. People choose the leaders they think will do the best job.

Reading Check **How do citizens choose government leaders?**

Vote For Smith

Government Leaders

Your city, state, and country each have a government leader. A **mayor** leads a city or town. A **governor** is the leader of a state. These leaders make sure people obey community and state laws.

The **President** is the leader of our country. This person makes sure people obey our country's laws. The President also works with the leaders of other countries to solve world problems.

Reading Check How are the jobs of the President, a governor, and a mayor alike?

Government Leaders		
Mayor	Governor	President
• Leads a city or town • Makes sure community laws are obeyed	• Leads a state • Makes sure state laws are obeyed	• Leads our country • Makes sure our country's laws are obeyed • Meets with world leaders

Children in History

Tutankhamen, Boy King

Not all leaders are adults. Long ago, Tutankhamen became the leader of Egypt when he was only eight years old. With the help of trusted adults, he ruled his country for ten years.

Summary Government leaders work to make our communities good places to live.

Review

1. **What to Know** Why do we need leaders?

2. **Vocabulary** How does a **mayor** help a community?

3. **Activity** Imagine you are the mayor of your city. Tell how you would help your community.

4. **Main Idea and Details** How are government leaders chosen?

Make a Choice by Voting

Why It Matters   In the United States, citizens choose their leaders by voting in elections. A **vote** is a choice that gets counted.

Learn

1 Before people vote, they think about who will do the best job.

2 People mark a ballot to vote in most elections. A **ballot** is a list of all the choices.

3 The ballots are counted.

4 The winner of an election is the one who gets the most votes.

Frieda

John

Usha

Tyler

28

Practice

Before Imagine that your classroom is a city that wants to choose a new mayor.

During Make ballots that list the name of each person who wants to be mayor. Give each citizen a ballot to mark.

After When everyone has voted, collect the ballots. The winner is the person who gets the most votes.

Frieda	John	Usha	Tyler
卌 I	卌 卌 卌	III	卌

Apply

Make It Relevant Use voting as a way to make other choices in your classroom.

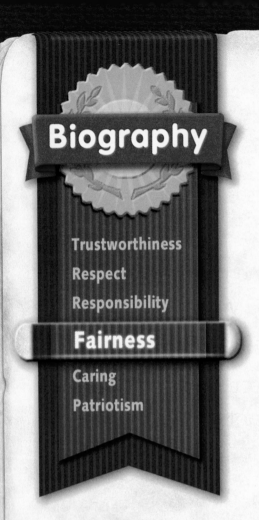

Trustworthiness

Respect

Responsibility

Fairness

Caring

Patriotism

Why Character Counts

How did Susan B. Anthony show fairness to other people?

Susan B. Anthony

Susan B. Anthony lived at a time when women did not have the same rights as men. Most girls did not go to school. They helped their mothers cook and clean at home. Susan's family felt that both girls and boys should be given an education.

Susan B. Anthony worked for equal rights.

Many women came together to work for women's rights.

For many years, women could not vote to help choose our country's leaders. Susan B. Anthony thought this was unfair, and she began to make speeches. She said, "It was . . . not we, the white male citizens . . . but we, the whole people, who formed the Union."

Susan B. Anthony worked hard giving speeches and writing books. Finally, 100 years after she was born, our country passed a law giving women the right to vote.

Susan B. Anthony was the first woman shown on United States money.

GO **ONLINE** For more resources, go to www.harcourtschool.com/ss1

Time

1820			1906
Born			Died

1839 Begins teaching school

1872 Arrested for voting in the Presidential election

1906 Makes her last speech for women's right to vote

Our Country's Government

Our country's government helps the United States run smoothly. The government has three parts, or branches. The legislative branch makes the laws. The executive branch sees that the laws are obeyed. The judicial branch makes sure the laws are fair.

What to Know
How does our country's government work?

Vocabulary
capital
Congress
Supreme Court
Constitution

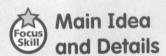

Main Idea and Details

Washington, D.C.

White House

The Capital

Washington, D.C., is the capital of our country. A **capital** is a city in which a state's or country's government meets and works.

The White House, which is the President's home, is in Washington, D.C. The Supreme Court and the Capitol building are also there.

(Reading Check) **What is the capital of the United States?**

Washington, D.C.

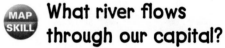

MAP SKILL **What river flows through our capital?**

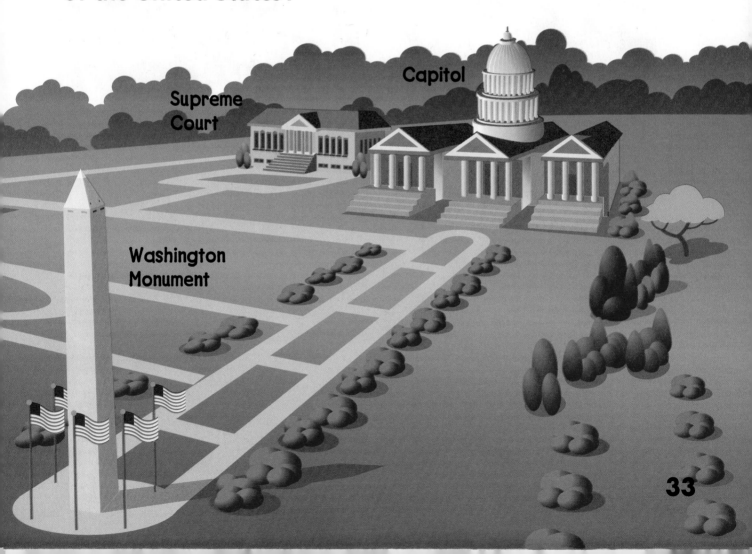

Supreme Court

Capitol

Washington Monument

The Legislative Branch

Congress is the lawmaking branch of our country's government. The people of each state elect their own members of Congress. Besides making laws, Congress also decides on the taxes people will pay.

Reading Check How are the members of Congress chosen?

The Executive Branch

The President is the leader of the executive branch. The executive branch sees that everyone obeys the laws Congress makes. The President can also suggest new laws to Congress.

Reading Check (Focus Skill) **Main Idea and Details** **What is the job of the executive branch?**

Fast Fact!

At the 1939 World's Fair in New York, Franklin D. Roosevelt became the first United States President to appear on television.

President Bush promises to work for the people.

The Judicial Branch

The judicial branch of the government makes sure that the laws are fair. The Supreme Court is part of the judicial branch. The **Supreme Court** decides on laws for the whole country.

The Supreme Court has nine judges. Each is chosen by the President and is agreed to by Congress. These judges make sure that laws are fair to all citizens.

Reading Check **What is the job of the Supreme Court?**

The Supreme
Court

The Constitution

The Constitution

The **Constitution** is a written set of rules that the government must follow. It explains how each branch of our government needs to work. The Constitution also lists the rights of all citizens of the United States. New rights and laws are added to the Constitution when they are needed.

Reading Check **Why does our government need the Constitution?**

Summary The three branches of our country's government follow the Constitution and work together for our country.

Review

1. **What to Know** How does our country's government work?

2. **Vocabulary** Why is the **Constitution** important?

3. **Activity** Make a chart showing the three branches of government and what they do.

4. **Main Idea and Details** What are some things to see in our country's capital?

Books for Everyone

One responsibility people have in their community is to work together to solve problems. The Constitution says that all people must have the same chances to do things. Read about some students who believed that everyone should have books to read.

Hollygrove is a home for children in southern California. When Brandon Keefe was in the third grade, he learned that the children at Hollygrove needed books for their library. He asked his class to help him solve this problem. Together they collected 847 books to give to the children at Hollygrove.

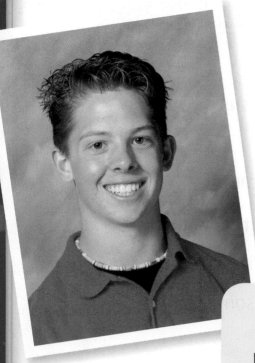

Brandon Keefe still works for BookEnds today.

Brandon's book drive grew into an organization called BookEnds. Volunteers collect used books so that all children can have a chance to read. Brandon says, "It's great to know you've made a difference and things are going to change because of what you've done."

Make It Relevant Why is it important to your community to help others learn how to read?

These children thank BookEnds for their new books!

Community and State Governments

A community and a state both have governments. These governments do different jobs for their citizens.

What to Know
What are the jobs of our community and state governments?

Vocabulary

council
legislature

Main Idea and Details

Boston Public Garden

Working for the People

Local governments work for the people of their community. They run the police and fire departments and plan buildings and parks.

State governments work for all the people in a state. They take care of state roads and highways. In an emergency, the state government helps people get the food and shelter they need.

Reading Check **How do community and state governments take care of citizens?**

The Legislative Branch

Like our country's government, state and community governments have three branches. A community's legislative branch is usually a city or town council. The **council** is a group of people chosen by citizens to make choices for them.

The council meets to talk about problems in the community and find solutions. In many communities, the council works with the mayor to make city laws.

Sam Bowman of the Oklahoma City City Council

The state legislature is like a community council, but it is much larger. A state's **legislature** is a group of elected citizens who makes decisions for the state. Each member represents a community in his or her state. Members of the legislature meet in the state capital to make laws.

(Reading Check) **In what ways are city councils and state legislatures alike?**

Representative Mary Waters of the Michigan State Legislature

Executive Branch

In both community and state governments, the executive branch makes sure that laws are obeyed. The executive branch of a community includes the mayor and other people who work to help the community's citizens.

Mayor Elaine Walker of Bowling Green, Kentucky

A state's executive branch includes the governor. The governor helps see that state laws are obeyed. He or she can also suggest new laws to the state legislature.

Reading Check **What is the job of the executive branches?**

Governor Mitch Daniels of Indiana

Judicial Branch

The judicial branches of both community and state governments are made up of the courts. The courts and the judges make sure city and state laws are carried out fairly.

Reading Check **What is the job of the judicial branches?**

Summary Like our country's government, community and state governments make laws and take care of citizens.

Review

1. **What to Know** What are the jobs of community and state governments?

2. **Vocabulary** What is the job of a state **legislature**?

3. **Activity** Make a poster to explain to your community council a law you think your community needs.

4. **Main Idea and Details** What is one of the jobs of a governor?

45

Read a Map Key

Why It Matters   The title of a map helps you know what the map will show. A **map key** explains what the symbols mean.

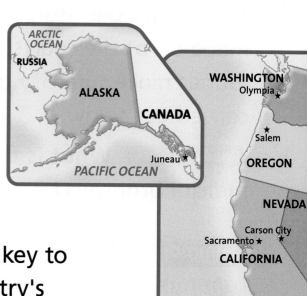

Learn

On this map, you can use the map key to find our national capital, or our country's capital. You can also use the key to find each state capital and borders. A **border** is a line that shows where a state or country ends.

Practice

❶ Find Kentucky on the map. What is the capital city?

❷ Which states are located on the borders of Oklahoma?

❸ Which states are located near our national capital?

United States

Apply

Make It Relevant Make a map of your state and the states located on its borders. Include a map key.

For online activities, go to
www.harcourtschool.com/ss1

Map Key

⊛ National capital

★ State capital

— Border

Field Trip

Read About

One of the best-known addresses in the United States is 1600 Pennsylvania Avenue. This is the address of the White House, in Washington, D.C. The President of the United States lives and works here.

People can take a tour of the 132 rooms of the White House. They can see furniture, artwork, and other things used by the past Presidents.

Find

United States

Washington, D.C.

THE White House

East Room

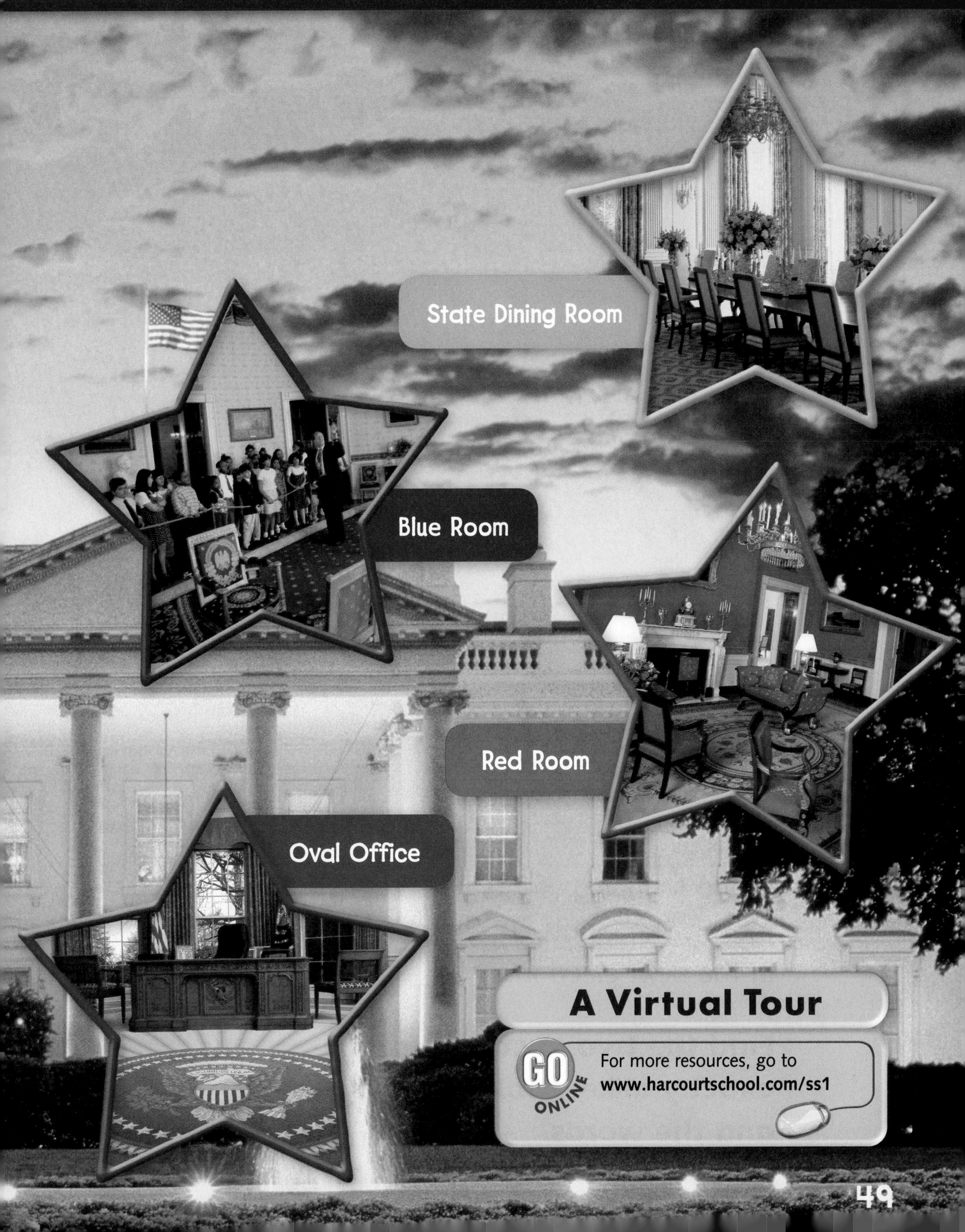

State Dining Room

Blue Room

Red Room

Oval Office

A Virtual Tour

GO
ONLINE

For more resources, go to
www.harcourtschool.com/ss1

It's a Match!

A

MARLA FOR MAYOR!

CHOOSE A GOOD LEADER
VOTE FOR MARLA

B

MARLA FOR MAYOR!

CHOOSE A GOOD MAYOR
VOTE FOR MARLA

Marla Manning wants to be the city's new mayor. She wants citizens to vote for her in the next election.

Find the two posters that are exactly alike. Look at the pictures and the words.

50

C

MARLA FOR MAYOR!

CHOOSE A GOOD LEADER
VOTE FOR MARLA

D

MARLA FOR MAYOR!

CHOOSE A GOOD LEADER
VOTE FOR MARLA

Online Adventures

GO ONLINE

Our country's capital is having a parade! Play an online game to help Eco find the parade and learn about government. Play now, at www.harcourtschool.com/ss1

Review and Test Prep

The Big Idea

Government A government makes laws to help people be safe and get along.

Focus Skill Main Idea and Details

Copy and fill in the chart to show what you learned about what a government does.

Main Idea

_____

_____

Details

| A government makes laws that citizens must follow. | People who break laws face consequences. | _____ _____ |

✔ Vocabulary

Fill in the blanks with the correct words.

My neighbor, Mrs. Arnold, likes to ① _____ in elections. By voting, she helps choose the people who run our community. This group of people, called a ② _____, helps everyone get along. Mrs. Arnold is a good ③ _____ in our community. She follows every ④ _____, or rule. I think she could someday be our country's ⑤ _____.

Word Bank

citizen
(p. 8)
law
(p. 11)
government
(p. 18)
President
(p. 26)
vote
(p. 28)

✔ Facts and Main Ideas

⑥ What kinds of rights do Americans have?

⑦ What is the job of a judge?

⑧ Why do citizens pay taxes?

⑨ What is the leader of a state called?
  A mayor   **C** judge
  B governor   **D** legislature

⑩ What is the lawmaking branch of our country's government called?
  A Supreme Court   **C** Congress
  B council   **D** President

⑪ Why do you think new laws have been added to the Constitution?

⑫ **Make It Relevant** What would happen if there were not consequences for breaking laws in your community?

Skills

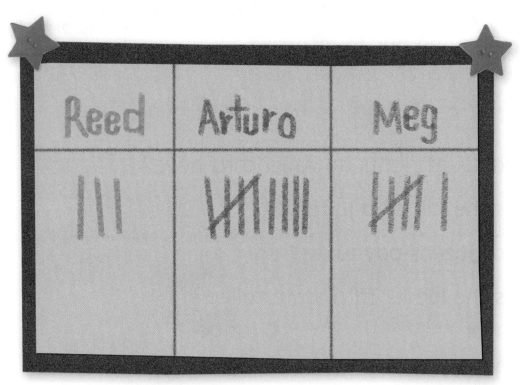

Reed	Arturo	Meg

⑬ Who has the fewest votes?

⑭ How many votes does Meg have?

⑮ How many votes does Arturo have?

⑯ Who has the most votes?

States in the South

WEST VIRGINIA
Charleston ★
Annapolis
⊛ ─MARYLAND
Washington, D.C.
Frankfort ★
KENTUCKY
VIRGINIA ★Richmond
OKLAHOMA
Oklahoma ★
City
ARKANSAS
Little ★
Rock
TENNESSEE ★Nashville
NORTH CAROLINA ★Raleigh
★Columbia
SOUTH CAROLINA
ALABAMA ★
MISSISSIPPI Atlanta
★ GEORGIA
TEXAS ★Jackson ★Montgomery
Austin ★
Baton
Rouge ★
LOUISIANA
★Tallahassee
FLORIDA
ATLANTIC OCEAN
Gulf of Mexico

North
West ━ East
South

Map Key
⊛ National capital
★ State capital
── Border

⑰ What is the capital city of Arkansas?

⑱ Which states share a border with North Carolina?

⑲ What state's capital is Frankfort?

⑳ What is the capital city of Tennessee?

55

Activities

Show What You Know

 Unit Writing Activity

Speak Out! What would help the citizens of your community stay safe?

Write a Letter Write a letter to the mayor about a problem. Tell how you think it should be solved.

 Unit Project

Role-Play Role-play how a city council makes laws.

- Practice presenting opinions.
- Use props and costumes.
- Role-play a council meeting and write a new law.

Read More

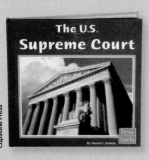

The U.S. Supreme Court
by Muriel L. Dubois

What Presidents Are Made Of
by Hanoch Piven

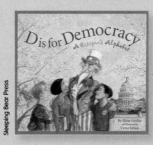

D is for Democracy: A Citizen's Alphabet
by Elissa Grodin

Community Government

All communities in Indiana have a government. The government in your community may have its own symbols. These symbols stand for your community and its customs. A symbol may be a flag or a seal. Your community may also have a motto that tells what is important to it.

What to Know
What is the government like in your community?

Vocabulary
allegiance p. IN I-2
republic p. IN I-2
volunteer p. IN I-5

Focus Skill Main Idea and Details

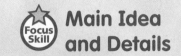

Flag of Cedar Lake, Indiana

Seal of South Bend, Indiana

The Pledge of Allegiance

The United States also has symbols. Each day, children in Indiana and all over the country stand and face the United States flag. Then they say the Pledge of Allegiance.

By saying the pledge, American citizens promise their **allegiance**, or loyalty, to the flag. They also promise loyalty to our republic. A **republic** is a kind of government in which people vote for leaders to make choices for them.

The Pledge of Allegiance

I pledge allegiance to the Flag
of the United States of America,
and to the Republic
for which it stands,
one Nation under God, indivisible,
with liberty and justice for all.

Reading Check **Main Idea and Details**

What do you promise when you say the Pledge of Allegiance?

Rights and Responsibilities

Like the United States, Indiana has a constitution. Indiana's constitution says that all citizens have equal rights. It also lists the rights of Hoosiers. Some of these rights are freedom of speech and the right to own property.

Citizens of Indiana and the United States also have responsibilities. They must serve on juries if they are asked. Adults also have a responsibility to vote in elections.

Citizens vote to choose their leaders.

Some Hoosiers take on other responsibilities. They **volunteer**, or work without pay to help others. Often Hoosiers volunteer to solve a community problem. Some might help clean up a river. Others might feed people who cannot buy enough food for their families.

Many Hoosiers choose to serve in the military. The Army, the Navy, the Air Force, and the Marine Corps are all parts of the military.

Hoosiers care for their community by collecting goods for food banks.

 Reading Check (Focus Skill) **Main Idea and Details**

What are two rights and two responsibilities of Hoosiers?

Veterans are honored in ceremonies.

Leaders in Indiana

Hoosiers work together in the state government. Indiana's governor leads the state. The General Assembly makes laws. The Senate and the House of Representatives make up this group. The Indiana Supreme Court is Indiana's highest court.

Most cities and towns in Indiana are led by a mayor. In many cities, laws are made by a city council. In towns, the town board makes laws.

Mayors give speeches to citizens.

Reading Check **Focus Skill Main Idea and Details**

Who leads most city governments?

Hoosiers talk to community leaders at town meetings.

Government Workers

There are different kinds of government workers. Teachers, mail carriers, and police officers are some kinds of government workers. All these workers provide services to Hoosiers.

Reading Check (Focus Skill) **Main Idea and Details**

Which government workers help you?

Schools are government services. Teachers help you learn.

A mail carrier delivers mail to the homes in a community.

Police officers make sure that people follow laws. They help keep people safe.

Good Citizens

Many famous Hoosiers have been good citizens. Abraham Lincoln was the sixteenth President. He was well known for being honest and fair. Long ago, Johnny Appleseed planted apple seeds in Indiana. He did this because he cared about people.

Reading Check (Focus Skill) **Main Idea and Details**

For what is Abraham Lincoln best remembered?

Summary All communities in Indiana have a government. All citizens of Indiana have rights and responsibilities.

Johnny Appleseed's real name was John Chapman.

Review

1 **What to Know** What is the government like in your community?

2 **Vocabulary** How is the United States a **republic**?

3 🖍 **Activity** Make a chart showing the leaders of your community and what they do.

4 (Focus Skill) **Main Idea and Details** What are some rights and responsibilities of citizens in your community?

The World Around Us

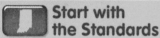

Start with the Standards

Indiana's Academic Standards for Social Studies

History 2.1.1, 2.1.2

Civics and Government 2.2.5

Geography 2.3.1, 2.3.2, 2.3.3, 2.3.4, 2.3.5, 2.3.6, 2.3.7

The Big Idea

The Land

Maps help us learn about the different kinds of land, water, and places around us.

What to Know

✓ How do maps help people find locations?

✓ What countries and landforms make up North America?

✓ Why are seasons and climate different in different regions?

✓ How are regions around the world different?

Communities in Indiana

Did You Know?

A boat ramp in Leavenworth connects the town to the Ohio River.

A community is a place where people live and work together. Hoosiers have built communities on different kinds of land in Indiana. East Chicago is a big city in northern Indiana. Leavenworth is a small town in southern Indiana.

East Chicago

East Chicago is located along Lake Michigan. The city's location allows people to ship goods and travel. Boats carry goods and people across Lake Michigan to the rest of the country.

East Chicago is a big city with many buildings and factories. A factory is a building in which people use machines to make goods. Some of these factories make steel.

Leavenworth is located on hilly land along the Ohio River. Hoosiers use the Ohio River to ship goods. They also visit the nearby Harrison Crawford State Forest.

Many Hoosiers in Leavenworth work in small factories or in shops. Because Leavenworth is a small community, its citizens often travel to larger communities to get what they need.

Stephenson's General Store

Indiana TEST PREP

1. How does East Chicago's location affect its citizens?
   A Hoosiers can travel across Lake Michigan.
   B Hoosiers can start farms.
   C Hoosiers cannot travel.
   D Hoosiers must work in factories.

2. Which body of water near Leavenworth do Hoosiers use to ship goods?
   A the Ohio River
   B Lake Michigan
   C Brookville Lake
   D the St. Joseph River

3. **Writing** How is your community like East Chicago or Leavenworth?

Unit 2

The World Around Us

Talk About
The Land

"People enjoy visiting Grandfather Mountain in North Carolina."

"My compass helps me use a map to find a location."

"It's fun to explore different landforms."

57

location The place where something is.

(page 66)

landform A kind of land with a special shape, such as a mountain, hill, or plain. (page 76)

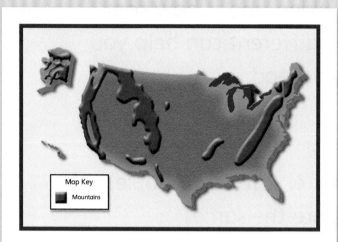

Map Key

Mountains

region An area of land with the same features.

(page 82)

cardinal directions The main directions of north, south, east, and west. (page 90)

climate The kind of weather a place has over a long time. (page 86)

GO ONLINE For more resources, go to www.harcourtschool.com/ss1

59

Reading Social Studies

Focus Skill

Compare and Contrast

Why It Matters Thinking about how some things are alike and different can help you understand what you read.

Learn

● To compare, think about how people, places, or things are the same.

● To contrast, think about how people, places, or things are different.

Read the paragraph below.

Compare

Contrast

Bryson City, North Carolina, and Baltimore, Maryland, are two cities in the United States. Visitors to Bryson City can hike in the mountains or float down the river in a raft. Baltimore is a good place to fish in the ocean or see old ships in a museum. In both cities, people can shop for gifts.

Bryson City

Baltimore

Practice

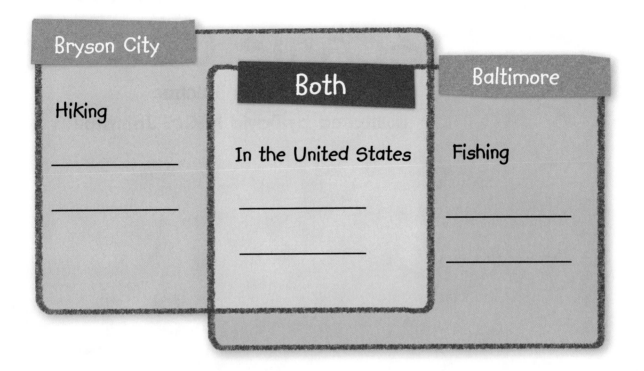

Bryson City

Hiking

_____

_____

Both

In the United States

_____

_____

Baltimore

Fishing

_____

_____

This chart shows how these two cities are the same and how they are different. What can you add to the chart? Copy the chart and complete it.

Apply

As you read this unit, look for ways to compare and contrast places where people live.

How the Prairie Became Ocean

by Joseph Bruchac

illustrated by David McCall Johnston

This story is a Native American legend. Legends are stories that teach a lesson or help explain something.

Long ago, when there were no people, the ocean was a treeless plain. Thunder stood and looked over the land. He knew that soon people would be there.

"How will the people be able to live?" Thunder turned to his companion, Earthquake. "What do you think?" Thunder asked. "Should we place water here?"

Earthquake thought. "I believe we should do that," he said. "Far from here, at the end of the land, there is water. Salmon are swimming there."

So Earthquake and Water Panther went to the end of the land, where there was ocean. They picked up two big abalone shells and filled the shells with salt water. Then they carried the shells back to Thunder.

Earthquake began to walk around. As he walked, the ground sank beneath him. Water Panther filled the sunken ground with the salt water.

Now there was ocean where there had only been a treeless plain. Thunder rolled over the mountains and bent the trees down so they would grow on the land. Seals and salmon and whales swam through gullies made by the sinking land.

Beside the ocean, the land rose up into hills and animals came down from the mountains— deer, elk, foxes, and rabbits.

"Now this will be a good place for the people to live," Thunder said.

"This is a good place," Earthquake agreed. "Let us live here, too."

And so, to this day, Thunder and Earthquake live there, near the place they made the land into ocean for the people.

Response Corner

1. (Focus Skill) **Compare and Contrast** How was the ocean different long ago?

2. **Make It Relevant** How are the landforms in this legend and the ones where you live alike and different?

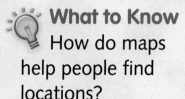
What to Know
How do maps help people find locations?

Vocabulary
location
relative location
absolute location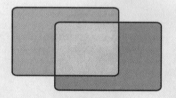

Focus Skill
Compare and Contrast

Maps and Locations

There are many kinds of maps. Maps show **location**, or the place where something is.

You can use maps to find the relative location of a place. The **relative location** tells what a place is near. On the map of Knoxville, the school is near the museum.

You can also use maps to find the absolute location of a place. The **absolute location** is the exact location. Your address is an absolute location. The absolute location of the library on this map is 500 West Church Avenue.

 MAP SKILL Which building on this map is closest to the river?

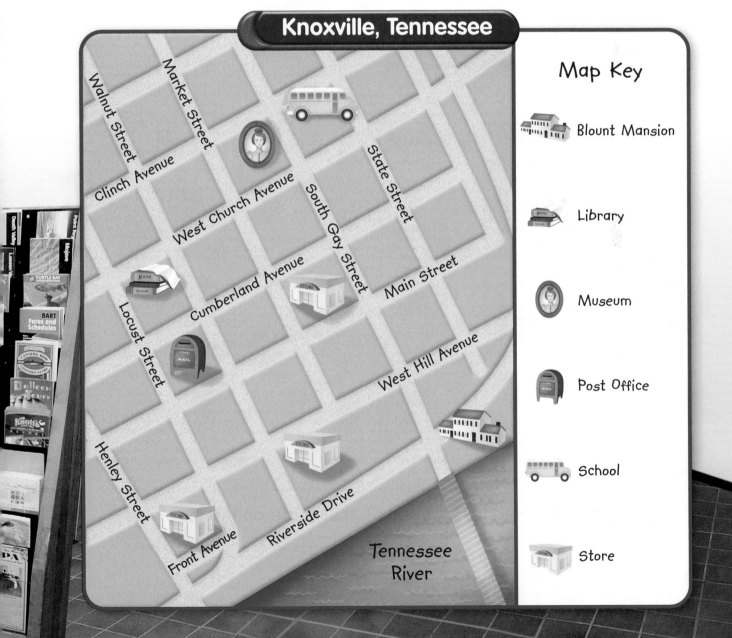

Knoxville, Tennessee

Walnut Street
Market Street
Clinch Avenue
West Church Avenue
South Gay Street
State Street
Cumberland Avenue
Locust Street
Main Street
West Hill Avenue
Henley Street
Front Avenue
Riverside Drive
Tennessee River

Map Key

Blount Mansion

Library

Museum

Post Office

School

Store

Different maps can show different kinds of information. Some maps show small areas, such as parks or neighborhoods. Other maps show large areas, such as cities, states, and countries.

United States

MAP SKILL What is the relative location of your state on this map?

The map shows that the city of Knoxville is in the state of Tennessee, in the country of the United States. The map also shows all of the states in our country.

Reading Check (Focus Skill) **Compare and Contrast**
How are the absolute location and the relative location of a place different?

Summary People use maps to help them find relative and absolute locations.

World's Fair Park in Knoxville, Tennessee

Review

1. **What to Know** How do maps help people find locations?

2. **Vocabulary** What is the **absolute location** of your home?

3. **Write** Make a map of your school. Write how to get from your house to your school.

4. (Focus Skill) **Compare and Contrast** How is the absolute location of your school different from its relative location?

Use a Map Grid

Why It Matters   A good way to find locations on a map is to use a map grid. A **map grid** is a set of lines that divide a map into columns and rows of squares.

Learn

columns

rows

❶ Put your finger on the gold square. Slide your finger left and right. This is row B.

❷ Put your finger on the gold square again. Slide your finger up and down. This is column 2.

❸ The gold square is at B-2 on the grid.

Practice

Look at the map grid of a park in Knoxville.

❶ In which square is Fort Kid?

❷ What place is in A-3?

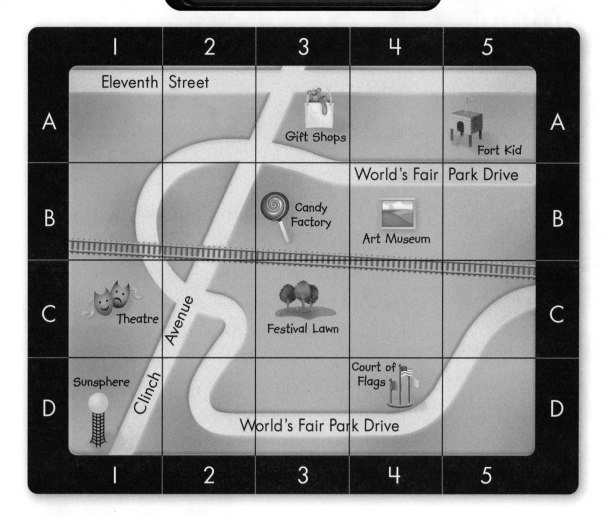

Apply

Use this grid map to find the absolute location of places in World's Fair Park. Have a classmate tell you the row and column of the square in which a place is located.

GO ONLINE

For online activities, go to **www.harcourtschool.com/ss1**

Trustworthiness

Respect

Responsibility

Fairness

Caring

Patriotism

Benjamin Banneker

When Benjamin Banneker was a young boy, he taught himself many things. He read books to learn about math. He studied the sky at night to learn about the stars. He even copied the parts of a watch and made a clock of his own. When he grew up, Benjamin Banneker became a writer and a scientist.

Why Character Counts

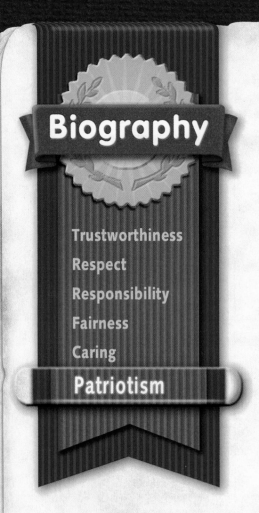 How did Benjamin Banneker show patriotism?

Benjamin Banneker helped measure the land for Washington, D.C.

This is an early map of Washington, D.C.

Banneker wrote almanacs that gave weather information and other useful facts.

In 1791, Benjamin Banneker was asked to help survey, or measure, a piece of land. On this land, the new capital of the United States government would be built.

President George Washington hired Benjamin Banneker to help map out the new city, Washington, D.C. His work helped build a grand city for the new American government.

For more resources, go to
www.harcourtschool.com/ss1

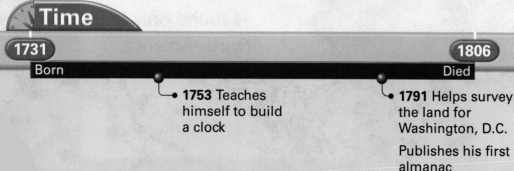

Time

1731		1806
Born		Died

1753 Teaches himself to build a clock

1791 Helps survey the land for Washington, D.C.

Publishes his first almanac

North America

The United States of America is the name of our country. Our country is located on the continent of North America.

What to Know
What countries and landforms make up North America?

Vocabulary

landform

peninsula

island

gulf

Focus Skill Compare and Contrast

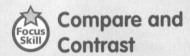

Countries in North America

There are many countries in North America. Canada and Mexico, our neighbors, are big countries. Central America has many smaller countries that are also part of North America.

Reading Check **Which two countries are neighbors of the United States?**

Fast Fact!

The bald eagle is found only in North America, in places from Florida and Mexico to Alaska and Canada.

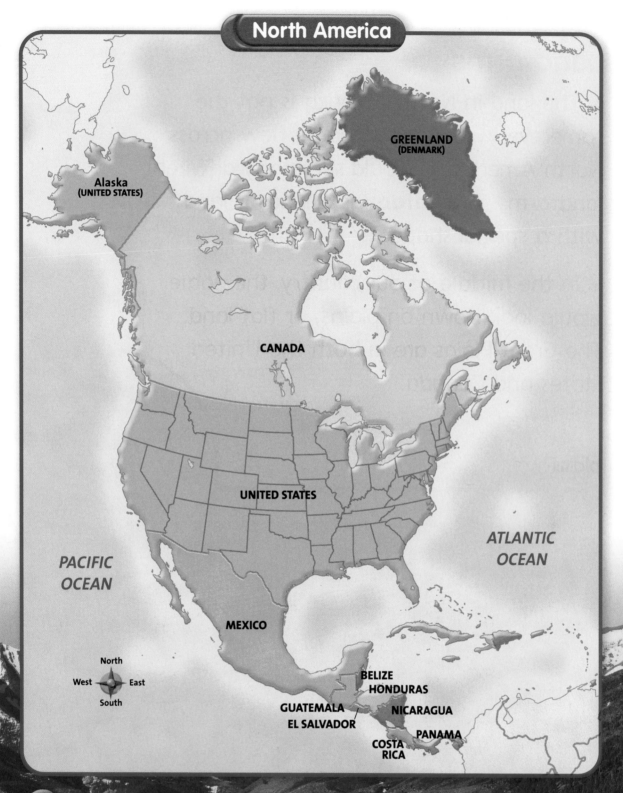

GREENLAND
(DENMARK)

Alaska
(UNITED STATES)

CANADA

UNITED STATES

PACIFIC
OCEAN

ATLANTIC
OCEAN

MEXICO

North

West — East

South

BELIZE
HONDURAS

GUATEMALA   NICARAGUA
EL SALVADOR

PANAMA

COSTA
RICA

MAP SKILL **Why is Alaska shown in the same color as the United States?**

Landforms

The land in North America is not the same everywhere. If an eagle flew across North America, it would see many different landforms. A **landform** is a kind of land with a special shape.

In the middle of our country, the eagle would look down on plains, or flat land. The Great Plains are in both the United States and Canada.

plains

wheat

hills

mountains

The eagle would also see land with many hills. A hill is land that rises above the land around it. A mountain is a very high hill. A group of mountains is called a mountain range. Many mountain ranges stretch across parts of North America.

Reading Check (Focus Skill) **Compare and Contrast**

How are plains different from hills?

Land and Water

Besides land, the eagle would fly over many kinds of bodies of water. The biggest are oceans. North America lies between two oceans.

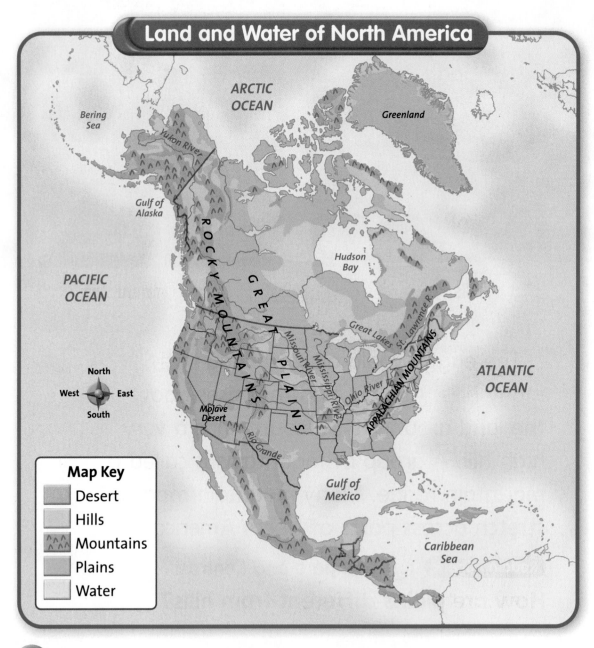

Land and Water of North America

ARCTIC OCEAN

Bering Sea

Greenland

Yukon River

Gulf of Alaska

PACIFIC OCEAN

Hudson Bay

ROCKY MOUNTAINS

GREAT PLAINS

Great Lakes

St. Lawrence R.

APPALACHIAN MOUNTAINS

ATLANTIC OCEAN

North
West — East
South

Missouri River

Mississippi River

Ohio River

Mojave Desert

Rio Grande

Gulf of Mexico

Caribbean Sea

Map Key
- Desert
- Hills
- Mountains
- Plains
- Water

 MAP SKILL Between which two oceans is North America located?

The eagle might fly over land that has water around it on only three sides. This landform is called a **peninsula**. The state of Michigan has many peninsulas.

An **island** is a landform with water all around it. Michigan also has many islands.

Michigan peninsula
in Lake Huron

Mackinac Island in Lake Huron

Sometimes a large body of water is partly surrounded by land. This body of water is called a **gulf**. The Gulf of Mexico is located between the United States and Mexico. A smaller body of water that is partly surrounded by land is called a bay.

Gulf of Mexico

Chesapeake Bay is surrounded by the states of Maryland and Virginia.

All over the land, there are rivers and lakes. A river is a stream of water that flows across the land. A lake is a body of water that has land all around it. The Great Lakes are large lakes located between the United States and Canada.

Reading Check **What kinds of bodies of water are there?**

Summary A map of North America shows countries, landforms, and bodies of water.

One of the longest rivers in North America is the Mississippi River.

Review

1. **What to Know** What countries and landforms make up North America?

2. **Vocabulary** What **landform** is located in the middle of the United States?

3. **Activity** Draw a map of North America. Label the countries, landforms, and bodies of water.

4. **Compare and Contrast** How are mountains different from hills?

81

Read a Landform Map

Why It Matters You can use a landform map to compare different regions of our country. A **region** is an area of land with the same features.

Learn

A landform map uses colors and symbols to show different kinds of land. Each kind of land makes up a region.

Practice

❶ Look at the map key. What kinds of land are shown on the map?

❷ Find the Great Lakes. What kind of land surrounds this region?

❸ What shows a mountain region on the map? Find and name the two biggest mountain ranges in the United States.

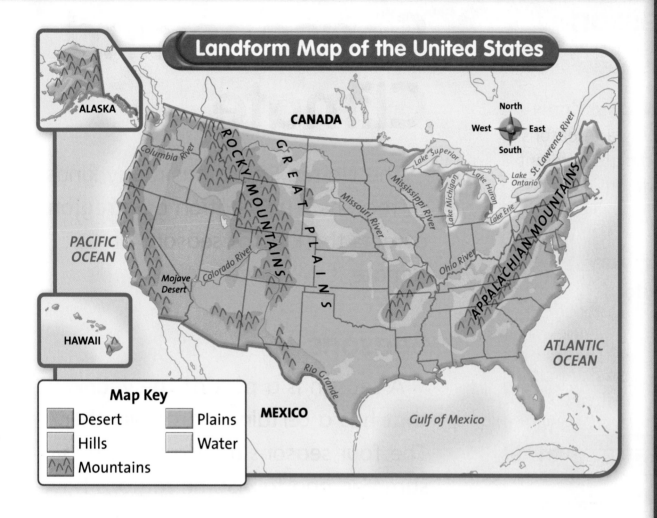

Landform Map of the United States

ALASKA

HAWAII

CANADA

Columbia River

ROCKY MOUNTAINS

GREAT PLAINS

Missouri River

Lake Superior

Lake Michigan

Lake Huron

Lake Ontario

Lake Erie

St. Lawrence River

Mississippi River

Ohio River

APPALACHIAN MOUNTAINS

North
West   East
South

PACIFIC OCEAN

Mojave Desert

Colorado River

Rio Grande

MEXICO

Gulf of Mexico

ATLANTIC OCEAN

Map Key
- Desert
- Hills
- Mountains
- Plains
- Water

Apply

Make It Relevant Use the map and key to describe the region in which you live. Compare your region to other regions of the United States.

GO ONLINE For online activities, go to **www.harcourtschool.com/ss1**

83

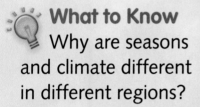
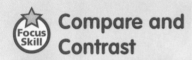 **What to Know**
Why are seasons and climate different in different regions?

Vocabulary
climate

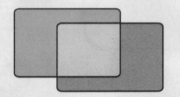 **Compare and Contrast**

Seasons and Climate

The United States has many kinds of regions. The location of a region affects the kind of seasons and climate it will have.

Seasons

A season is a part of the year that has a certain kind of weather. The four seasons are winter, spring, summer, and fall. Some regions have four very different seasons. Other regions have the same kind of weather all year long.

A warm summer day in Boston, Massachusetts

The season a place is having depends on how Earth is facing the sun. Earth circles the sun in a tilted position. It is summer in places that are tilted toward the sun. It is winter in places that are tilted away. As Earth travels, different parts of it are tilted toward the sun. This causes the seasons to change.

Reading Check **Why do the seasons change?**

summer

winter

Weather and Climate

In each region, the weather can change from day to day. Weather is the way the air feels outside. One day the weather might be sunny and warm. Another day it might be cloudy and cool.

Climate is the kind of weather a place has over a long time. Many mountain regions have a cool climate. People there need to dress warmly. Some desert regions have a warm climate. There, people wear clothes to keep themselves cool.

Reading Check (Focus Skill) **Compare and Contrast How is weather different from climate?**

Carmel, Indiana, has many snowy days.

Smoky Mountains

Arizona desert

Summary The location of a place affects the weather, climate, and seasons it will have.

Review

1 **What to Know** Why are seasons and climate different in different regions?

2 **Vocabulary** What is the **climate** like where you live?

3 ✏ **Write** Write sentences that compare and contrast the weather of two different seasons where you live.

4 (Focus Skill) **Compare and Contrast** How can a mountain climate be different from a desert climate?

87

Read a Table

Why It Matters A **table** is a chart that organizes information. Knowing how to read a table can help you remember information.

Learn

The title tells you what the table shows. Put your finger on the first square of a row. Read the information. The column labels tell the kinds of information you see.

Practice

❶ What does the table show?

❷ What are the column labels?

❸ What was the high temperature for May?

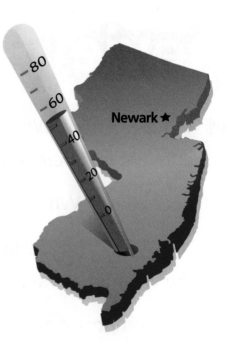

Temperatures in Newark, New Jersey		
Month	High Temperature	Low Temperature
January	38°	23°
February	41°	25°
March	51°	33°
April	62°	43°
May	72°	53°
June	82°	63°
July	87°	69°
August	85°	67°
September	78°	60°
October	67°	48°
November	55°	39°
December	43°	30°

Apply

Make It Relevant   Make a table that shows high and low temperatures of where you live.

GO ONLINE   For online activities, go to
www.harcourtschool.com/ss1

World Regions

What to Know
How are regions around the world different?

Vocabulary

cardinal directions

equator

pole

hemisphere

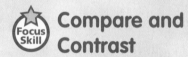

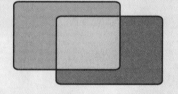

Focus Skill **Compare and Contrast**

A globe is a model of Earth. We can use the **cardinal directions**—north, south, east, and west—to find locations on a globe and on Earth.

The Equator, Poles, and Hemispheres

The **equator** is an imaginary line that divides Earth into northern and southern halves. Regions near the equator are very hot.

Equator

A **pole** is a point on Earth farthest from the equator. The farthest you can travel north from the equator is the North Pole. The farthest you can travel south is the South Pole. The regions close to each pole are very cold.

A **hemisphere** is half of Earth. The equator divides Earth into the Northern and Southern Hemispheres.

(Reading Check) How would a region near a pole be different from a region near the equator?

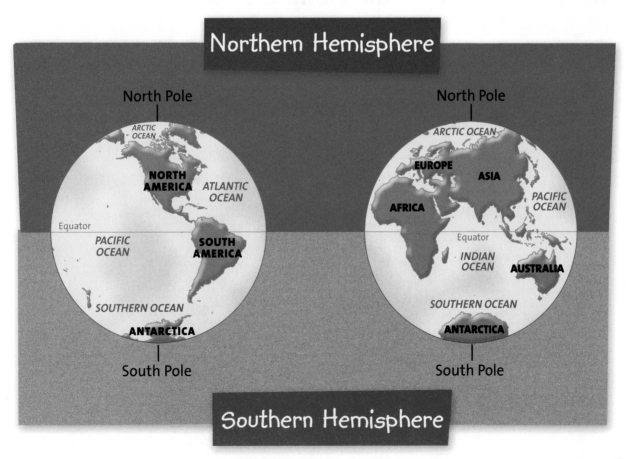

Features of World Regions

The world has many different regions. Each region has its own landforms and climate. A mountain region might be cold and snowy, with rocky land. A tropical region near the equator might be warm and flat, with plenty of rain.

Each region has animals and plants that live and grow there. People use what they have in a region to help them live.

Reading Check **Compare and Constrast**

How are regions of the world the same?

Tropical Region

Rain forest in Brazil

92

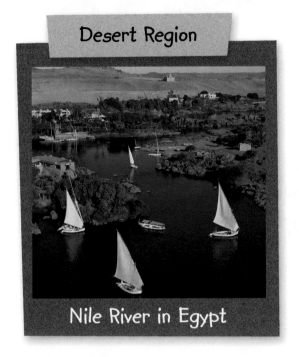

Desert Region

Nile River in Egypt

Mountain Region

Himalayas in Nepal

Summary There are many kinds of regions in different locations on Earth. Each region has its own landforms and climate.

Review

1. **What to Know** How are regions around the world different?

2. **Vocabulary** Where would you find the **poles** on a globe?

3. **Activity** Draw a picture of a world region. Show its climate, landforms, plants, and animals.

4. (Focus Skill) **Compare and Contrast** How is a mountain region like a tropical region? How are these two regions different?

Find Directions on a Map

Why It Matters Directions help you describe where places are on a map or globe.

Learn

A **compass rose** shows directions on a map or globe. **Intermediate directions** are between the cardinal directions. They are northeast, northwest, southeast, and southwest.

Practice

❶ What country is our neighbor to the north?

❷ What country is our neighbor to the south?

❸ In which direction would you travel to go from Greenland to Mexico?

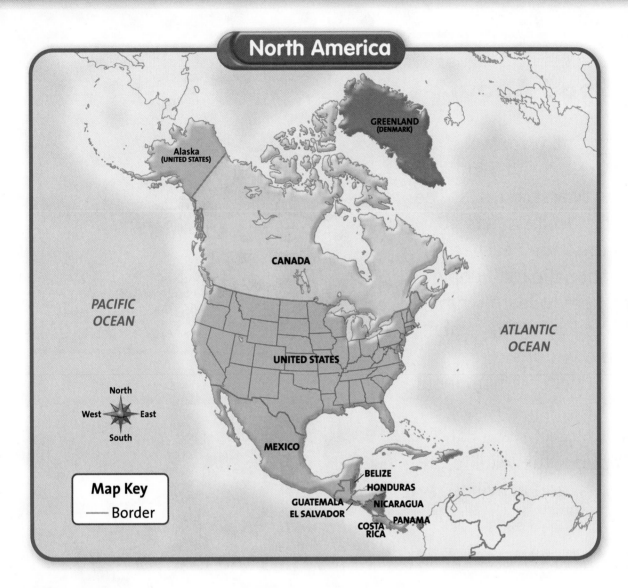

North America

GREENLAND
(DENMARK)

Alaska
(UNITED STATES)

CANADA

PACIFIC
OCEAN

ATLANTIC
OCEAN

North

West — East

South

UNITED STATES

MEXICO

Map Key
—— Border

BELIZE
HONDURAS
GUATEMALA   NICARAGUA
EL SALVADOR
                   PANAMA
COSTA
RICA

Apply

Make It Relevant Find some places on
a map of your state. Use cardinal and
intermediate directions to tell how to
get from place to place on the map.

GO ONLINE For online activities, go to
www.harcourtschool.com/ss1

Field Trip

Read About

Cape Cod National Seashore is located in eastern Massachusetts. The Atlantic Ocean meets 40 miles of sandy beaches at this national park. People come here to learn what it is like to live in this region.

At the visitor's center, you can watch a film about Cape Cod. There is also a museum where you can learn about the wildlife, buildings, and activities at the park.

Find

United States

Cape Cod National Seashore, Massachusetts

Cape Cod National Seashore

Highland Lighthouse

Children can take part in the Junior Ranger Program to learn more about the national park.

Biking is a popular activity at the park.

There are many kinds of wildlife at Cape Cod National Seashore.

White Cedar Swamp

A Virtual Tour

GO
ONLINE

For more resources, go to
www.harcourtschool.com/ss1

Find the winning line.

Will the winner be Summer or Winter?

Missing Letters

Each word is missing the same letter. When you find it, use the letter to answer the riddle.

Clue	Word
the place where something is	l o c / t i o n
a landform with water all around it	i s l / n d
the kind of weather a place has	c l i m / t e
an imaginary line that divides Earth	e q u / t o r

What islands are good to eat?

The S / n d w i c h   I s l / n d s

Review and Test Prep

 The Big Idea

The Land Maps help us learn about the different kinds of land, water, and places around us.

Focus Skill Compare and Contrast

Copy and fill in the chart to show how a desert region and mountain region can be alike and different.

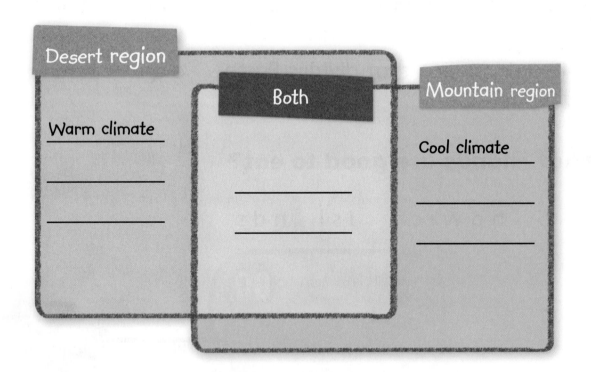

Desert region

Warm climate
_____
_____
_____

Both
_____
_____

Mountain region

Cool climate
_____
_____
_____

100

Vocabulary

Match the word to its meaning.

1 a kind of land with a special shape

2 the kind of weather a place has over a long time

3 an area of land with the same features

4 the place where something is

5 the main directions of north, south, east, and west

Word Bank

location
(p. 66)
landform
(p. 76)
region
(p. 82)
climate
(p. 86)
cardinal
directions
(p. 90)

Facts and Main Ideas

6 What kind of location is your address?

7 Which continent is our country a part of?

8 What kind of landform has water all around it?

9 Which of these is a part of the year with its own kind of weather?

   A season   **C** hemisphere

   B climate   **D** region

10 What is the imaginary line that divides Earth into northern and southern halves?

   A pole   **C** compass rose

   B continent   **D** equator

⑪ How does knowing the relative location help you find a place?

⑫ **Make It Relevant** How might your family trips be different if you did not have maps?

Skills

Average Rainfall		
City	Winter rainfall	Summer rainfall
Little Rock, Arkansas	12 inches	10 inches
Louisville, Kentucky	20 inches	12 inches
Baltimore, Maryland	10 inches	12 inches
Wilmington, North Carolina	12 inches	20 inches
Tulsa, Oklahoma	6 inches	11 inches

⑬ What does this table show?

⑭ What are the column labels?

⑮ Which city had the most winter rainfall?

⑯ Which city had the most summer rainfall?

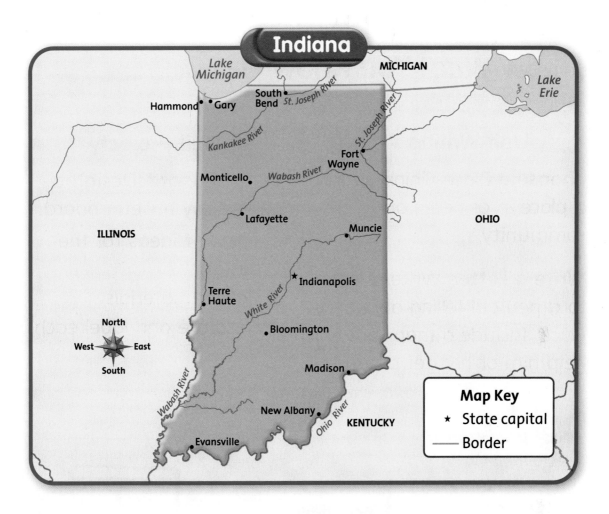

Indiana

⑰ In which direction would you go to get from Evansville to Terre Haute?

⑱ Which cities on this map are southwest of Indianapolis?

⑲ Which state is north of Indiana?

⑳ Which state is west of Indiana?

Show What You Know

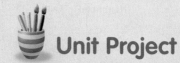

✏️ Unit Writing Activity

Choose a Place Think about a place in or near your community.

Write a Letter Write a letter to a pen pal telling about the place. Include a map that will help him or her get around.

🖌️ Unit Project

Bulletin Board Design a geography bulletin board.

- Think of ideas for the design.
- Gather materials.
- Decorate and label each section.

Read More

Ideals Children's Books

The Whole World in Your Hands: Looking at Maps
by Melvin and Gilda Berger

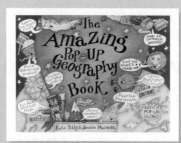

Dutton Children's Books

The Amazing Pop-Up Geography Book
by Kate Petty and Jennie Maizels

Reader's Digest Children's Books

Way to Go! Finding Your Way with a Compass
by Sharon Sharth

GO ONLINE
For more resources, go to
www.harcourtschool.com/ss1

The Land of Indiana

Can you find Indiana on the map of North America? First, find the United States. Then look for the Great Lakes. Next, find the Ohio River. Indiana is south of Lake Michigan. It is north of the Ohio River.

MAP SKILL Which bodies of water border Indiana?

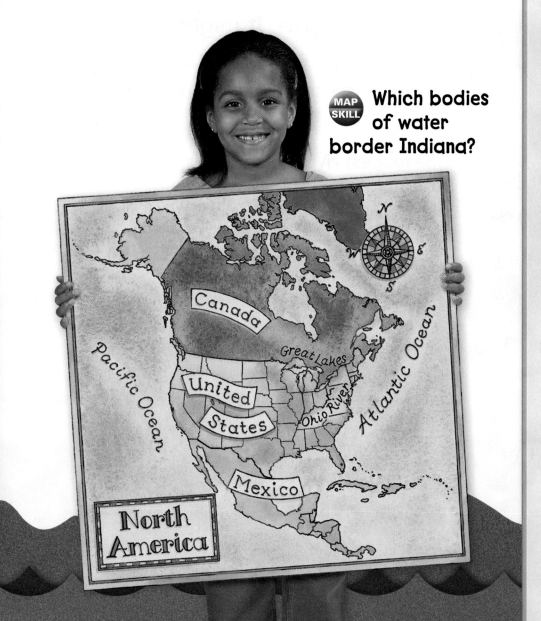

Vocabulary
plains p. IN 2-2

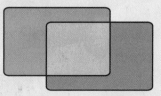

Focus Skill Compare and Contrast

Many farms in Indiana are on plains.

Indiana's Land and Water

What would the eagle see if it flew over Indiana? In the north, it would see Lake Michigan. This is one of the Great Lakes. In the middle of the state, it would see flat land, or **plains**. Then the eagle would see hills in the south. Finally, it would see the Ohio River.

Along the way, the eagle might see other sights. It might look down on forests and farms. It might also see lakes and rivers.

The longest river in Indiana is the Wabash River.

Look at the map below. What kinds of land do you see?

What lakes and rivers can you name? Now find where you live. What are the land and water like around there?

Reading Check **Compare and Contrast**

How does the land change from north to south in Indiana?

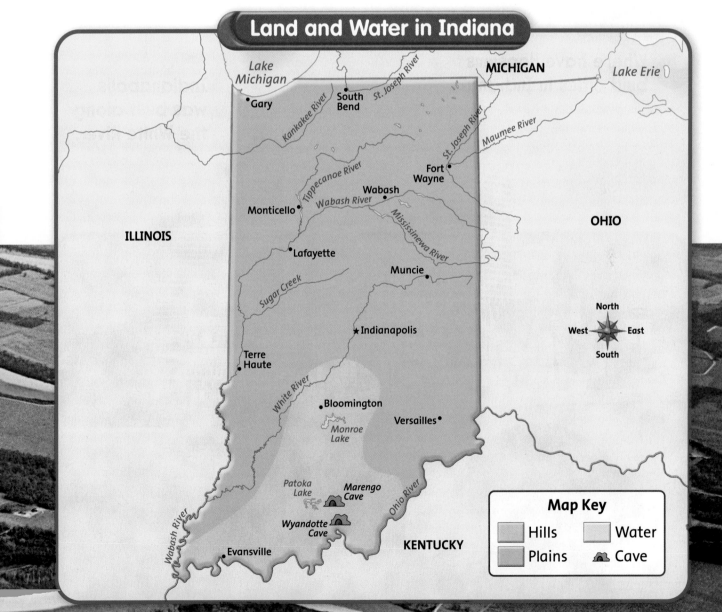

Land and Water in Indiana

Lake Michigan

MICHIGAN

Lake Erie

Gary

South Bend

St. Joseph River

Kankakee River

St. Joseph River

Maumee River

Fort Wayne

Tippecanoe River

Wabash

Wabash River

Monticello

Mississinewa River

ILLINOIS

OHIO

Lafayette

Muncie

Sugar Creek

North

West — East

South

★ Indianapolis

Terre Haute

White River

Bloomington

Versailles

Monroe Lake

Patoka Lake

Marengo Cave

Ohio River

Map Key

Hills   Water

Wyandotte Cave

KENTUCKY

Plains   Cave

Wabash River

Evansville

People Change the Land

Over time, people have changed the land in Indiana. They have made roads and highways. They have also built houses and other buildings. Hoosiers have cleared land for farms. They have also built bridges across lakes.

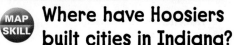

MAP SKILL **Where have Hoosiers built cities in Indiana?**

Indianapolis was built along the White River.

Many roads and buildings Hoosiers have made are part of cities and towns. Some cities are big. They have a downtown area and many neighborhoods. Indiana's largest cities are Indianapolis, Fort Wayne, Evansville, and South Bend.

Look at the map of downtown Indianapolis. Find the Soldiers' and Sailors' Monument. Identify other buildings in Indianapolis. Indianapolis has many houses, stores, offices, and restaurants. The city also has large parks.

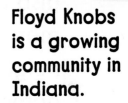

Floyd Knobs is a growing community in Indiana.

Reading Check **How have Hoosiers changed the land in Indiana?**

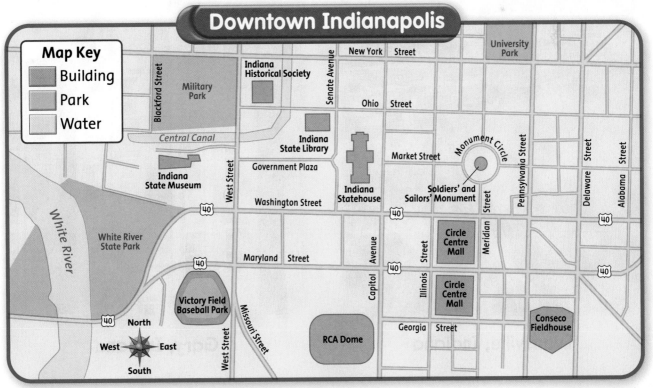

Downtown Indianapolis

Map Key
- Building
- Park
- Water

Communities and Neighborhoods

Indiana has different kinds of communities. The land and water in a community can affect the way people live there. The Ohio River helped Evansville become an important trade center.

Neighborhoods in a community may also be different. The city of Gary has more than ten neighborhoods. One neighborhood is known for its many old homes. Another has Art Deco buildings.

Evansville, Indiana

Gary, Indiana

Most neighborhoods in Indiana have their own schools. This means that children can go to school near where they live. Other children ride buses to go to schools in nearby neighborhoods.

Schools can be different in each neighborhood. Is your school big or small? How many girls are in your class? How many boys? How many classrooms are in your school?

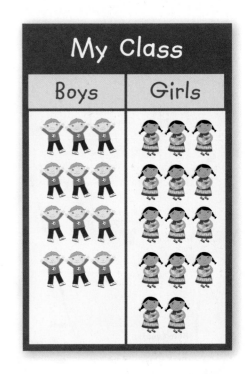

Reading Check **Compare and Contrast**

How is your community like the communities you read about?

Children of many cultures go to school in Indiana.

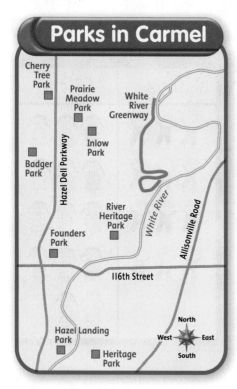

Parks in Carmel

Cherry Tree Park
Prairie Meadow Park
White River Greenway
Hazel Dell Parkway
Inlow Park
Badger Park
River Heritage Park
White River
Allisonville Road
Founders Park
116th Street
North
West — East
South
Hazel Landing Park
Heritage Park

MAP SKILL Near which body of water is Hazel Landing Park?

Green Spaces

Many neighborhoods have green spaces. These are open areas near homes, schools, and community buildings. Some green spaces are woods. Others are parks near lakes and rivers.

Reading Check What green spaces are in your community?

Summary Indiana has plains and hills. Hoosiers have changed the land by building roads, cities, and neighborhoods.

Review

① **What to Know** What kinds of land and water are in Indiana?

② **Vocabulary** Where would you find **plains** in Indiana?

③ ✎ **Write** Make a map of the land and water in your community. Write how they affect the way you live.

④ (Focus Skill) **Compare and Contrast** How are northern Indiana and southern Indiana different?

Using Our Resources

Start with the Standards

Indiana's Academic Standards for Social Studies

History 2.1.2

Civics and Government 2.2.5

Geography 2.3.2, 2.3.3, 2.3.4, 2.3.5, 2.3.7

Economics 2.4.1, 2.4.4

The Big Idea

Resources
People use the land and its resources to help them live.

What to Know

✔ What natural resources do people use? How do they use them?

✔ What are some of the reasons people choose to live in a place?

✔ How do people change their environment?

✔ How have transportation and communication changed over time?

Recreation in Indiana

Did You Know?

The Indiana bat was discovered in the Wyandotte Caves.

Indiana's land and water affect what Hoosiers do for recreation. Recreation is any activity that is done for fun. Hoosiers can use Indiana lakes and rivers for boating. They can use hills and forests for hiking.

Some communities are near hills and forests. The O'Bannon Woods State Park is in Corydon. Hoosiers go to the park to hike on the hills and to ride horses.

Chain O' Lakes State Park, in northern Indiana, borders three lakes. It also borders the Fox River. This river connects to seven other lakes. Visitors can fish in the lakes.

Some communities are near rivers. Harmonie State Park is near the Wabash River in New Harmony. Hoosiers can go there to swim in the river. They can also swim in the park's pool.

Also in O'Bannon Woods State Park are the Wyandotte Caves. These caves are made of limestone. Visitors can explore these caves, which are sometimes called underground mountains.

Indiana ✓ TEST PREP

1. How do Hoosiers use lakes in Indiana?
   A to fish
   B to bike
   C to explore caves
   D to hike

2. Which state park is located in Corydon?
   A Shades
   B O'Bannon Woods
   C Harmonie
   D Whitewater Memorial

3. **Writing** What types of recreation do you do in your community?

Using Our Resources

Talk About

Resources

" Our food is grown in Earth's rich soil. "

Preview

Vocabulary

natural resource Something found in nature that people can use. (page 114)

conservation The saving of resources to make them last longer.

(page 118)

technology The use of new objects and ideas in everyday life. (page 134)

product Something that is made by nature or by people. (page 136)

For more resources, go to www.harcourtschool.com/ss1

Reading Social Studies
Focus Skill
Cause and Effect

Why It Matters Knowing why things happen can help you understand what you read.

Learn

● What makes something happen is a cause.

● What happens is the effect.

Read the paragraph below.

Effect

Cause

Green beans come from bean plants. I grew my own beans! I filled a cup with soil. I pressed bean seeds into the soil and waited. The seeds did not grow because I forgot to water them. Then I watered my seeds carefully. They began to grow. When the bean plants got bigger, I planted them outside.

Practice

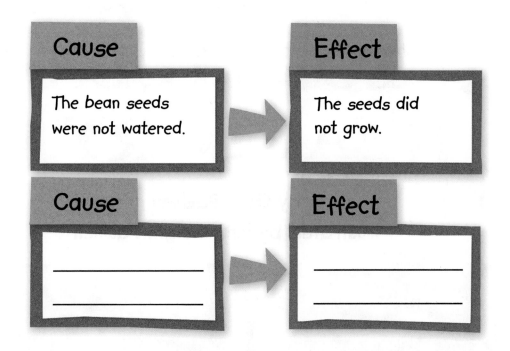

Cause		Effect
The bean seeds were not watered.	→	The seeds did not grow.

Cause		Effect
_____ _____	→	_____ _____

This chart shows what happened to the seeds and why it happened. Copy the chart and complete it.

Apply

As you read this unit, look for the ways people change the land where they live. Find out what causes these changes.

THE TORTILLA FACTORY

by Gary Paulsen

illustrated by Ruth Wright Paulsen

The black earth sleeps
in winter.
But in the spring the
black earth is worked by
brown hands that plant
yellow seeds, which become
green plants rustling in
soft wind and make golden
corn to dry in hot sun and
be ground into flour

for the tortilla factory,
where laughing people
and clank-clunking
machinery mix the flour
into dough,
and push the dough,
and squeeze the dough,
and flatten the dough...

...and bake the dough
into perfect disks that
come off the machine
and into a package
and onto a truck and
into a kitchen

to be wrapped around juicy beans
and eaten by white teeth, to fill a round stomach
and give strength to the brown hands
that work the black earth
to plant yellow seeds,

which make golden corn to be dried
in hot sun and be ground into flour...

Response Corner

1. **(Focus Skill) Cause and Effect** What causes the flour to turn into dough?

2. **Make It Relevant** How do farmers help you?

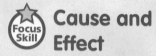
What to Know

What natural resources do people use? How do they use them?

Vocabulary

natural resource

fuel

conservation

Cause and Effect

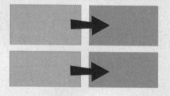

Land and Water Resources

People use natural resources to live. A **natural resource** is something found in nature that people can use.

People Use Air

People, plants, and animals need clean air to live. Some people use moving air to bring power to their homes. A wind turbine uses the wind's energy to produce electricity.

Reading Check **How do people use air?**

114

People Use Water

People use water for drinking, cooking, cleaning, and growing plants for food. Like air, water can also be used to produce electricity. In some dams, water produces electricity by flowing through and turning big machines.

Wolf Creek Dam, Kentucky

Reading Check **How do people use water?**

Wind Turbines

People Use Land

Another natural resource is land. We grow plants and build houses on land.

Trees are a very useful natural resource. Some farmers grow trees that make fruits and nuts. People use wood from trees to build furniture and homes. They also use wood to make paper.

Under the ground, people can find other natural resources, such as coal, oil, and natural gas. People dig and drill for these resources and make them into fuel. A **fuel** is a resource that can be burned for heat or energy.

(Reading Check) **How do people use land?**

Caring for Our Resources

With so many people living on Earth, we must protect our resources. **Conservation** is the saving of resources to make them last longer. Recycling is another way to save resources. When we recycle, we use something again in a new way.

Communities help care for resources by recycling.

If we do not take care of our natural resources, they can become dirty. Anything that makes the air, land, or water dirty is called pollution. Clean air, water, and land help all living things stay healthy.

Reading Check (Focus Skill) **Cause and Effect**

How does conservation help protect our resources?

Summary Natural resources give us what we need to live.

Recycling food garbage can keep soil healthy.

Review

① **What to Know** What natural resources do people use? How do they use them?

② **Vocabulary** What are two kinds of **fuel**?

③ ✏️ **Write** Think about all of the resources you use in one day. Then write a short paragraph about how you can conserve one of the resources.

④ (Focus Skill) **Cause and Effect** What would happen if we didn't take care of our natural resources?

Read a Picture Graph

Why It Matters   A **picture graph** makes information easier to understand by using pictures to show numbers of things.

Learn

The picture graph on the next page shows how much water Jen's family uses in one day. The key shows that each picture stands for five gallons of water.

Practice

❶ How much water did Jen's family members use to brush their teeth?

❷ For what did they use the most water?

❸ Did Jen's family use more water to wash dishes or to flush the toilet?

120

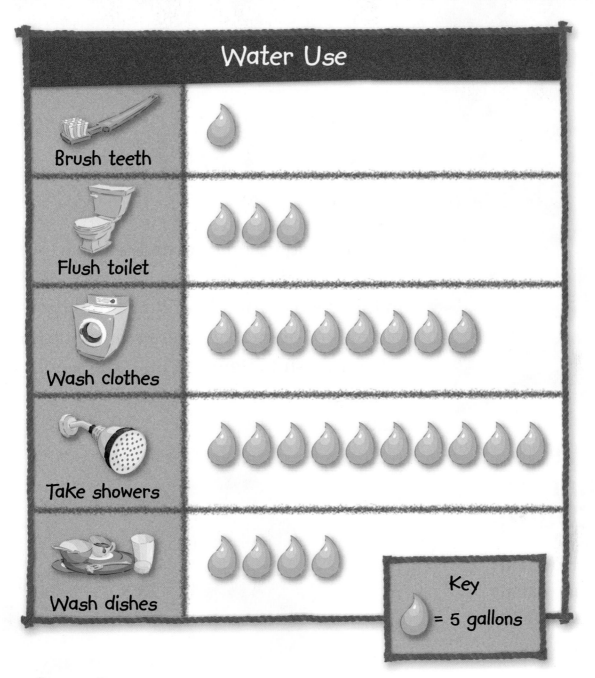

Water Use

Brush teeth	💧
Flush toilet	💧💧💧
Wash clothes	💧💧💧💧💧💧💧💧
Take showers	💧💧💧💧💧💧💧💧💧💧
Wash dishes	💧💧💧💧

Key
💧 = 5 gallons

Apply

Make It Relevant   Make a picture graph to show how much water your family uses in a day.

GO ONLINE For online activities, go to
www.harcourtschool.com/ss1

Trustworthiness

Respect

Responsibility

Fairness

Caring

Patriotism

Rachel Carson

Growing up on a farm, Rachel Carson loved the outdoors. She played in the woods around her home and drew pictures of animals. "There was no time when I wasn't interested in … the whole world of nature," Rachel Carson later said.

Why Character Counts

How did Rachel Carson show that she cared about nature?

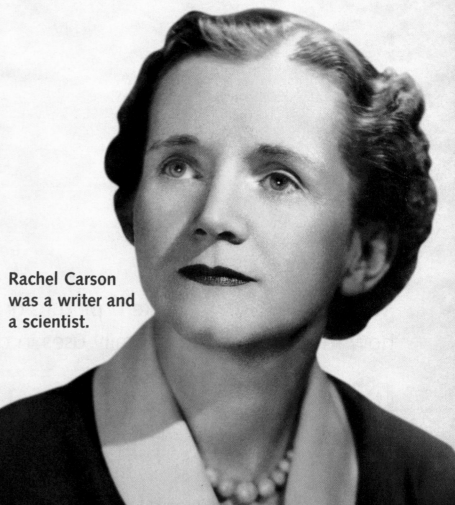

Rachel Carson was a writer and a scientist.

Rachel Carson grew up in the country and loved to be outdoors.

Rachel Carson also liked to write about the beauty of birds, plants, and the ocean. Then she began to notice that some people were doing things that hurt nature.

In 1962, she wrote a book called Silent Spring. In it, she told people about the dangers of pesticides, or poisons used to kill insects. These pesticides were also killing birds and plants. Because of Rachel Carson's book, better laws were made to keep nature safe.

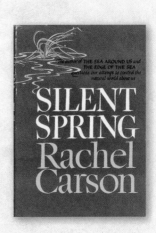

GO ONLINE
For more resources, go to www.harcourtschool.com/ss1

Time

1907
Born

1964
Died

1918 Writes her first story, at the age of ten

1936 Works as a biologist for the United States government

1962 Writes her most famous book, Silent Spring

Lesson  2

What to Know
What are some of the reasons people choose to live in a place?

Vocabulary

rural
urban
suburb

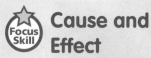
Cause and Effect

People Settle

Choosing a Place to Live

All people need food, water, and shelter. In some places, these things are hard to get. It is hard to grow food on rocky mountains. Deserts do not get enough rain for drinking water. Long ago, people could not choose to live in places like these.

In some places, people can find the natural resources they need. The flat, rich lands of the Great Plains are good for growing food. Rivers provide fish and water.

Once people decide to live in an area, they start to build the things they need. They build roads and bridges to make it easier to get from place to place. They make homes for shelter. Communities begin to grow.

Reading Check **Why would people want to live by a river?**

Rural Areas

Communities can be different sizes. Kendra lives on a soybean farm in a rural area in Indiana. **Rural** areas are usually in the country, far away from a city. People's homes may be far apart. Kendra has to travel by car to visit her neighbors.

People who live in rural areas can use the natural resources there to grow food and raise animals. They use wood from the trees for building homes. Many people in rural areas also sell resources and products to people in other places.

Reading Check (Focus Skill) **Cause and Effect Why do many people in rural areas grow food and raise animals?**

Children in History

Elfido Lopez

Elfido Lopez was born in Colorado in 1869. His family used the natural resources of the area to build a new home. The miles of wild grass fed their oxen. When he was older, Elfido learned how to cut down the wheat they grew. The river waters turned a millstone to crush their wheat into flour.

Urban Areas and Suburbs

Michael lives in the city of Indianapolis, Indiana. A city is an **urban** area. Urban areas have many businesses, homes, and people.

Elena lives in Avon, a suburb of Indianapolis. A **suburb** is a smaller community near a city. It has quieter neighborhoods, less traffic, and bigger yards.

Avon, Indiana

Indianapolis, Indiana

128

This map shows where people live in Indiana. The map key can help you find where rural, urban, and suburban areas are.

Reading Check **Why do some people live in suburbs?**

Summary People have settled in places with good natural resources. These places can be rural, urban, or suburban areas.

People in Indiana

Lake Michigan
MICHIGAN
Indian Village
Gary
Portage
South Bend
Warsaw
Fort Wayne
Monticello
INDIANA
OHIO
Lafayette
Kokomo
Attica
Muncie
ILLINOIS
Avon
Richmond
★Indianapolis
Terre Haute
Columbus
Bloomington
Washington
Bedford
North
Salem
Princeton
Jeffersonville
New Albany
West
East
Evansville
Newburgh
South
KENTUCKY

Map Key
Most people
Many people
Fewest people

MAP SKILL **Where do most people live in Indiana?**

Review

1. **What to Know** What are some of the reasons people choose to live in a place?

2. **Vocabulary** How is a **suburb** different from a city?

3. **Activity** Make a poster about your community. Show things that are natural and things people have made.

4. **Focus Skill** **Cause and Effect** What can cause an urban city to be a busy place to live?

Note Taking

Why It Matters Notes are important words and sentences that help you remember what you read.

Learn

Kevin used the learning log on the next page to take notes on the paragraph below. He wrote words and sentences from the paragraph under Note Taking. He wrote his own thoughts under Note Making.

Practice

Read the paragraph below. Add your own notes to the learning log.

The corn grown in Ohio is used for many things. It is used to feed animals. It can be made into cooking oil, flour, and sweeteners. Toothpaste and glue also have corn in them. Corn can even be turned into fuel for cars and machines!

Learning Log

Note Taking	Note Making
Corn is grown in Ohio.	Corn is grown in my state.
Corn is used for many things.	Corn is in many of the foods I eat and things I use.
_____	_____
_____	_____

Apply

Make a learning log about using our resources. As you read more about resources, add notes to your learning log.

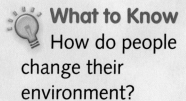
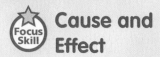
Vocabulary
environment
technology

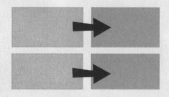 **Cause and Effect**

Changing Our Environment

The **environment** is all of the things that people find around them. People change their environment to meet their needs and make life easier.

Farming Long Ago

People long ago had to change the land before they could plant crops. They cut down trees, dug out stumps, and moved rocks. Then they plowed the land so they could plant seeds.

People faced many problems growing crops long ago. Rabbits, mice, and bugs ate the young plants. Weather was also a problem. Sometimes there would be no rain for a long time, and the plants would die. Bad storms could also kill the plants.

Reading Check **What problems did farmers face growing crops long ago?**

Farming Today

Farmers used technology to solve the problems they had growing crops. **Technology** is the use of new objects and ideas in everyday life. Better tools make planting and harvesting crops faster and easier. In dry weather, today's farmers use pipes and sprayers to bring water to crops.

Reading Check **How does new technology help farmers grow more crops?**

Long ago, people planted seeds by hand. Today, machines plant many seeds at a time.

Future Farming

In the future, farming may use less of one natural resource. Hydroponics is a kind of farming that does not use soil. Plants grow in water that has the minerals in it that they need. Pumps move air and water around the roots.

Reading Check **Focus Skill** Cause and Effect

What is an effect of using hydroponics?

Hydroponics

floating plants

air line

roots

air pump

Summary People use technology to change their environment to meet their needs.

Review

1 **What to Know** How do people change their environment?

2 **Vocabulary** Name a **technology** farmers use.

3 **Activity** Make a poster that shows how people have changed the environment in your community.

4 **Focus Skill** **Cause and Effect** What effect has new technology had on farming?

Read a Product Map

Why It Matters   Some maps show the resources and products of a place. A **product** is something made by nature or by people.

Learn

A **product map** uses symbols to show where resources and products are found or made. The map on the next page shows some of the resources and products of Arkansas.

Practice

❶ What products are shown in the map key?

❷ What animals are raised in Arkansas?

❸ Where in Arkansas is oil found?

136

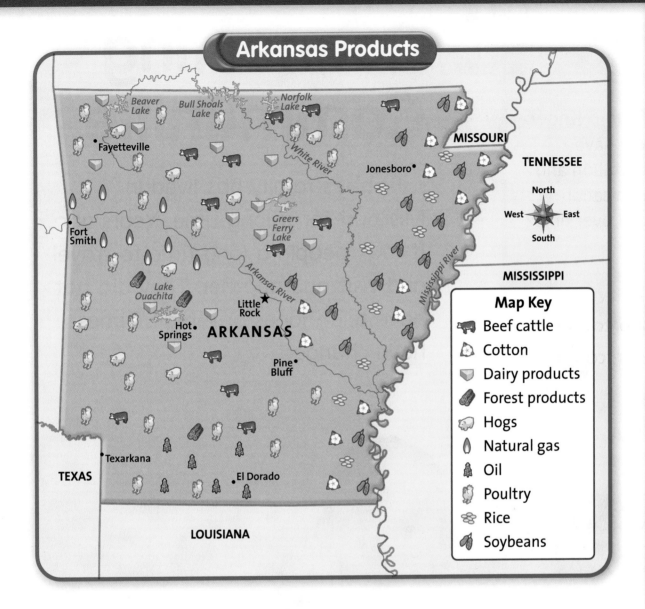

Arkansas Products

Map Key
- Beef cattle
- Cotton
- Dairy products
- Forest products
- Hogs
- Natural gas
- Oil
- Poultry
- Rice
- Soybeans

Apply

Make It Relevant Think of a product from your state. What symbol would you use for it on a product map?

For online activities, go to
www.harcourtschool.com/ss1

Connecting Communities

What to Know
How have transportation and communication changed over time?

Vocabulary
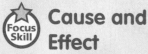
transportation
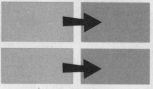
communication

Focus Skill Cause and Effect

Bobby's family has lived in Missouri for a long time. Years ago, it took people a long time to travel and visit one another. They did not have telephones or e-mail. Times have changed.

Going Places

Transportation is the moving of goods and people from place to place. Long ago, Bobby's family used horses to pull wagons on dirt roads. Transportation was very slow, and it was not easy to cross certain landforms.

Technology has made transportation faster and easier. Now there are paved roads and cars. Bobby flies in a plane to visit relatives far away.

Reading Check **How is transportation today different from long ago?**

St. Charles, Missouri

SPEED LIMIT 15

Communication Changes

Communication is the sharing of ideas and information. Liz's grandparents live in China. Even though China is far away, Liz's family can keep in touch with them by letters, telephone, and e-mail.

Long ago, people could only write letters to friends and family who lived far away. Their letters had to travel over land or by ship. This could take a long time.

Technology has created new ways of communication that connect people. Today, television, radio, and the Internet let us know what is happening all over the world.

Reading Check **What are some ways of communication people use today?**

Summary New ways of transportation and communication connect people more easily.

Review

1 **What to Know** How have transportation and communication changed over time?

2 **Vocabulary** What is one tool that has made **communication** faster?

3 **Activity** Make a chart to compare and contrast ways of transportation and communication of long ago and today.

4 **Cause and Effect** What has caused communication to change over time?

Follow a Route

Why It Matters   A map can show you where places are and how to get to them.

Learn

The path you follow from one place to another is called a **route**. Highways are routes between towns and cities. A compass rose tells you in which direction you are going when you follow a route.

Practice

❶ Which highway goes from Oklahoma City to Tulsa?

❷ In which direction would you travel on Highway 44 to go from Oklahoma City to Lawton?

❸ Which river does Highway 60 cross?

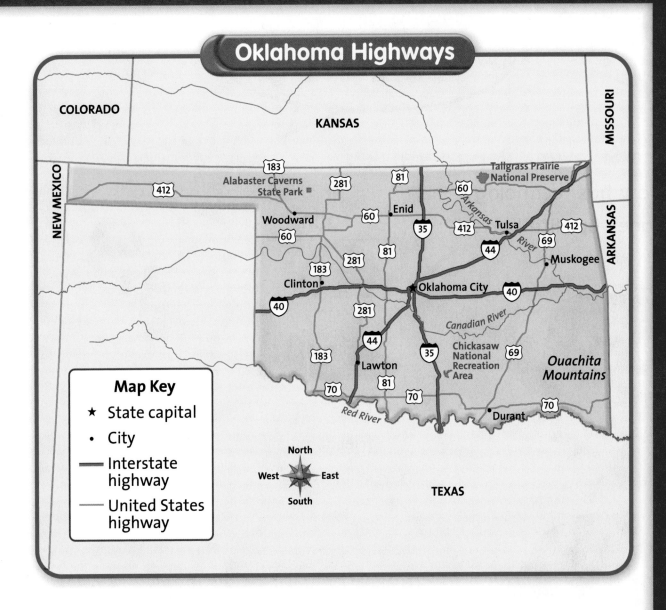

Oklahoma Highways

COLORADO

KANSAS

MISSOURI

NEW MEXICO

Tallgrass Prairie
National Preserve

Alabaster Caverns
State Park

ARKANSAS

Woodward

Enid

Tulsa

Muskogee

Clinton

Oklahoma City

Canadian River

Lawton

Chickasaw
National
Recreation
Area

Ouachita
Mountains

Red River

Durant

Map Key

★ State capital

• City

—— Interstate highway

—— United States highway

North

West ✦ East

South

TEXAS

Apply

Make It Relevant Draw a map to show your route to school. Add a compass rose to show directions.

GO ONLINE

For online activities, go to
www.harcourtschool.com/ss1

Points of View

The Sidewalk Reporter asks:
"How has technology made your life better?"

John

"I can call my friends on my cell phone."

Latisha

"I can do my homework on the computer."

View from the Past

Johannes Gutenberg: Communication

Long ago, books were written by hand, so there were not many of them. In about 1450, Johannes Gutenberg invented a way to print books faster. This let more people share ideas.

Carrie

"I can take an airplane to visit my grandmother."

Mr. Perez

"My grandson writes e-mails to me, but I also like it when he sends me a card in the mail."

Mrs. Patel

"I can buy frozen food at the store."

It's Your Turn

- Do any of these kinds of technology make a difference in your life? If so, which ones?
- What other kinds of technology have made your life easier or better?

Fun With Social Studies

What Doesn't Belong?

Look at the picture of an urban area. Find seven things that belong in a rural area.

146

Online **GO** Adventures

Play the online game to help Eco's class find ways to save a community park. You will need to use what you know about resources. Play now, at www.harcourtschool.com/ss1

Review and Test Prep

 The Big Idea

Resources People use the land and its resources to help them live.

Cause and Effect

Copy and fill in the chart to show what you have learned about why people use natural resources.

Using Natural Resources

Cause	Effect
Water turns big machines in dams.	The machines produce electricity.
Farmers grow trees.	_____ _____
_____ _____	_____ _____

Vocabulary

Complete each sentence.

① We can protect our resources by using _____.

② New _____, such as tools and machines, helps farmers grow more crops.

③ A _____ is something made by nature or by people.

④ Water is an important _____ that people can use to make electricity.

Word Bank

natural resource
  (p. 114)
conservation
  (p. 118)
technology
  (p. 134)
product
  (p. 136)

Facts and Main Ideas

⑤ How can people use air as a natural resource?

⑥ What do we do when we recycle?

⑦ Why did few people live in the desert long ago?

⑧ What is a smaller community near a city called?

⑨ Which kind of transportation was used long ago?
  A horse and wagon   C car
  B plane   D motorcycle

⑩ What is the sharing of ideas and information?
  A pollution   C transportation
  B communication   D conservation

⑪ Why do different places use their natural resources in different ways?

⑫ **Make It Relevant** What would happen if no one recycled or conserved resources in your community?

Skills

Money Earned from Recycling

Plastic bottles	$1 $1 $1
Cans	$1 $1 $1 $1
Glass bottles	$1 $1
Paper	$1

Key
$1 = $1

⑬ What does this picture graph show?

⑭ Which kind of item earned the most money?

⑮ How much money was earned from recycling glass bottles?

⑯ Was more money earned from recycling paper or glass bottles?

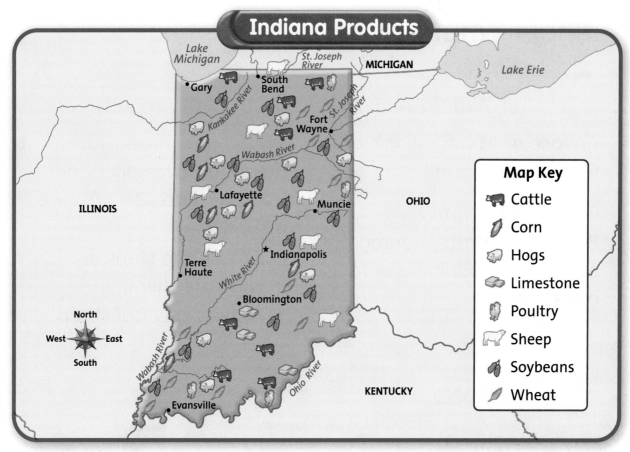

Indiana Products

Map Key
- Cattle
- Corn
- Hogs
- Limestone
- Poultry
- Sheep
- Soybeans
- Wheat

17 What does this map show?

18 What crops are grown in western Indiana?

19 What kinds of animals are raised in Indiana?

20 Where in Indiana are most sheep raised?

Show What You Know

Unit Writing Activity

Choose a Product Think of a farm product you like.

Write a Descriptive Paragraph Write a paragraph about the product. Give facts and details.

Unit Project

Earth's Resources Flowchart Create a flowchart about using resources to produce a food.

- Explain the steps and illustrate them.
- Answer any questions.

Read More

Holiday House, Inc.

The Great Trash Bash by Loreen Leedy

Copper Beech

Food and Farming by Pam Robson

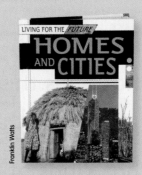

Franklin Watts

Homes and Cities: Living for the Future by Sally Morgan

GO ONLINE For more resources, go to www.harcourtschool.com/ss1

People Long Ago

Start with the Standards

Indiana's Academic Standards for Social Studies

History 2.1.1, 2.1.2, 2.1.3, 2.1.4, 2.1.5, 2.1.7

Civics and Government 2.2.1, 2.2.5, 2.2.6

The Big Idea

History

History is the story of how people and places change over time.

What to Know

✔ How do people and places change over time?

✔ What do we know about the people who lived in North America long ago?

✔ How did our country get its independence?

✔ How do we honor our American heritage?

✔ How do we honor people and events in our country's history?

Famous Hoosiers

Indiana has been home to many leaders and businesspeople. Many writers and artists are also from Indiana. These people have added to the history and culture of Indiana and the United States. They are also important to the communities from which they come.

Did You Know?

Abraham Lincoln grew up in Indiana from the age of seven. You can visit the farm where he lived. It is now called the Lincoln Boyhood National Memorial.

Abraham Lincoln moved to Indiana when he was seven years old. He became President of the United States in 1861. As President, he helped end slavery. Lincoln City is named for him.

Madam C.J. Walker started a business that sold beauty products. In 1910, Walker moved her business to Indianapolis. She later opened schools and gave money to people in need.

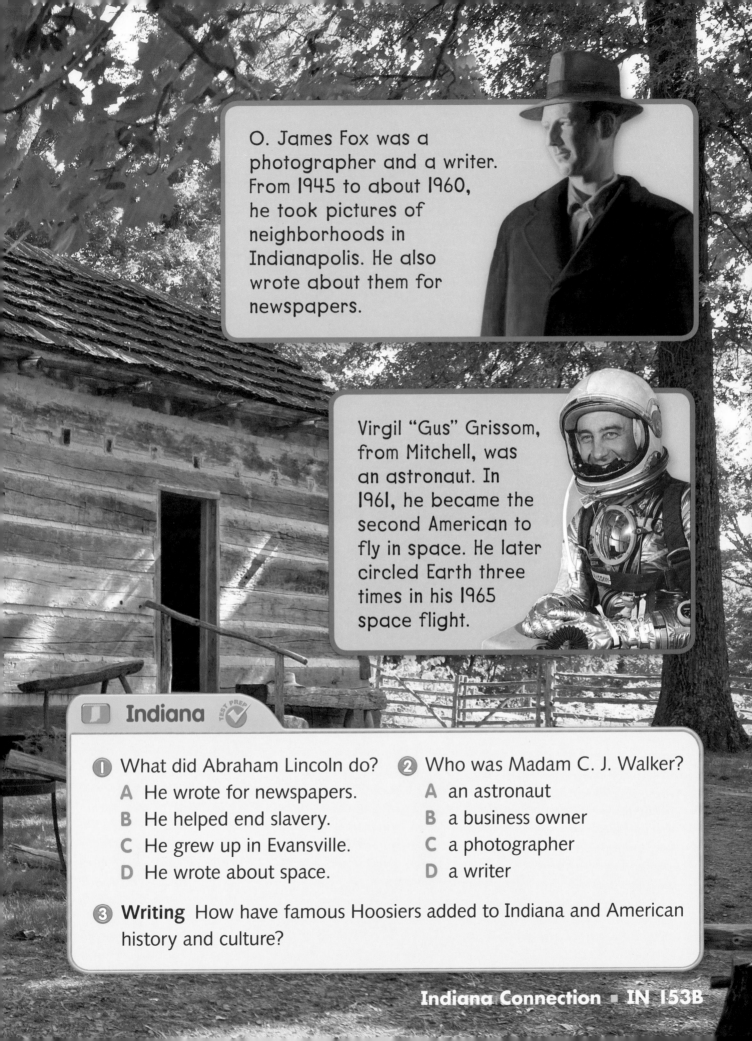

O. James Fox was a photographer and a writer. From 1945 to about 1960, he took pictures of neighborhoods in Indianapolis. He also wrote about them for newspapers.

Virgil "Gus" Grissom, from Mitchell, was an astronaut. In 1961, he became the second American to fly in space. He later circled Earth three times in his 1965 space flight.

Indiana TEST PREP

1. What did Abraham Lincoln do?
   A He wrote for newspapers.
   B He helped end slavery.
   C He grew up in Evansville.
   D He wrote about space.

2. Who was Madam C. J. Walker?
   A an astronaut
   B a business owner
   C a photographer
   D a writer

3. **Writing** How have famous Hoosiers added to Indiana and American history and culture?

People Long Ago

Talk About

History

"I like to visit Fort McHenry in Baltimore, Maryland, to learn about a time in our country's history."

"The bald eagle is a symbol of freedom."

"Voting is an important part of being a citizen in our country."

Vocabulary

change What happens when something becomes different.
(page 174)

history The study of things that happened in the past. (page 178)

colony   A place that is ruled by another country. (page 180)

landmark   A feature that makes a location special. (page 197)

independence   The freedom of people to choose their own government. (page 187)

GO
ONLINE

For more resources, go to
www.harcourtschool.com/ss1

Reading Social Studies

Focus Skill

Sequence

Why It Matters Knowing the sequence, or the order, in which events happen helps you understand what you read.

Learn

As you read, look for the words <u>first</u>, <u>next</u>, and <u>last</u>. These words give sequence clues.

Read the paragraph below.

Sequence   Anna Maria's grandfather moved to Oklahoma when he was 20 years old. First, he built a small house. Next, he found a job on a ranch. Grandfather fixed fences and helped with the cattle. Last, he used the money he saved to buy his own ranch. Anna Maria now lives in the house that her grandfather built long ago.

Practice

First

Grandfather built a small house.

Next

_____

_____

_____

Last

_____

_____

_____

This chart shows the sequence of events in Grandfather's life. What happened first? What happened next? What happened last? Copy the chart and complete it.

Apply

As you read, look for words that give sequence clues for events.

When I Was Young

by James Dunbar

illustrated by Martin Remphry

Josh likes visiting Grandma Jenny.
Her apartment is full of her memories.

"What was it like when you were
young, Grandma?" asks Josh.

And Grandma Jenny says—

When I was young, we lived in a new house and got our first TV. We had a kitchen with an electric stove and a fridge. Grandpa Ben used to visit us on weekends. My sister used to dress up and go dancing every Saturday night.

I remember asking Grandpa
what it was like when he was
young. And Grandpa Ben said—

When I was young, in England, my mum
and dad worked in a big hotel. Dad used
to polish the carriages. Sometimes he let me
feed the horses. I saw a car in the street
for the first time.

I remember the first time we had our photo taken. This is me in my sailor suit with mum, dad, my brother, Ted, my sister, May, Grandpa Jim, and Grandma Emily.

I asked Grandma Emily what it was like when she was young. Grandma Emily sat me on her knee and said—

When I was young, I remember playing in the street with all the other children. At night, I used to get scrubbed in a bathtub in the kitchen. We had candles for lighting.

We lived in a busy town.
Grandfather Joe used to take
me to the docks. We watched
the big ships from all around
the world come and go.

I used to ask Grandfather what it was like when he was young. Grandfather Joe sat me on his knee and said—

When I was young, I lived in the country. My father and grandfather worked on a farm.

At harvesttime everybody helped, even my Grandmother Polly.

Two days each week, we went to the village school. The teacher was very strict.

I remember asking my grandmother what it was like when she was young. Grandmother Polly sat me on her knee and said—

When I was young, I used to help my older sister, who worked at a big house. Downstairs in the kitchen, I polished candlesticks and scrubbed the tables and helped prepare the food. Upstairs in the large rooms, I dusted the furniture and helped make the fire.

I remember the fair coming to town.
There were games and dancing and
market stalls.

I used to ask my grandfather what it was like when he was young. Grandfather Will sat me on his knee and said—

When I was young, we traveled to all the country markets where my father and grandfather bought and sold horses.

I remember Grandmother Betty making dolls and small toys. They were made from wood. I used to help paint the faces. She gave one of the wooden dolls to me . . .

I remember thinking, "When I am as old as Grandmother Betty, I will tell my grandchildren what it was like when I was young."

Betty
Born in 1648

Will
7 years old in 1697

Polly
7 years old in 1744

Joe
7 years old in 1796

Ben
7 years old in 1899

Emily
7 years old in 1848

Jenny
7 years old in 1952

Josh

Response Corner

1. **Focus Skill** **Sequence** Who was born first, Grandma Jenny or Josh?

2. **Make It Relevant** Find out what life was like for an older relative when he or she was your age.

171

1

People and Places Change

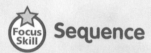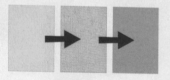
Focus Skill Sequence

Past, Present, and Future

Katie Britt lives with her parents and grandparents in Marietta, Ohio. Katie's grandparents remember the **past**, or the time before now. The clothes they wore then look different. Some of the work people did and the ways they had fun were different, too. Some are still the same.

Katie thinks about what her family and community are like right now in the **present**. She also likes to think about what her life will be like in the future. The **future** is the time yet to come. Katie knows she will be different but will still like to do things with her family.

Reading Check **What words name the parts of time in order?**

Changes Over Time

A **change** happens when something becomes different. Long ago, Marietta, Ohio, looked different. Over time, more people have moved into the community. New houses and roads have been built. Technology has also changed the way people live.

Marietta, Ohio, past and present

Putnam Street, 1950s

Places in a community may change over time, but people in the present still do some of the same things as people in the past. They still go shopping in stores and eat in restaurants. Families still enjoy playing in parks.

Reading Check (Focus Skill) **Sequence What changes happen after more people move into a community?**

Summary People and places change over time.

Review

1. **What to Know** How do people and places change over time?

2. **Vocabulary** Describe a **change** that you have seen in your school or community.

3. ✏️ **Write** Look at pictures and news articles from the past. Write about the ways things were different then from the ways they are today.

4. (Focus Skill) **Sequence** Which happens first, the future or the past?

Read a Diagram

Why It Matters   A **diagram** is a picture that shows the parts of something. A family tree is a diagram that shows the parts of a family.

Norma
Brown

Warren
Brown

Louise
Britt

Robert
Britt

Michelle
Brown

James
Britt

Katie
Britt

Learn

This family tree gives information about Katie Britt's family. It shows Katie, her parents, and her grandparents.

Practice

❶ Where can you find the youngest people on a family tree diagram?

❷ Who are the people in the middle row of Katie's family tree?

❸ What are the names of Katie's grandparents?

Apply

Make It Relevant   Make a family tree that shows the members of your family.

For online activities, go to
www.harcourtschool.com/ss1

What to Know
What do we know about the people who lived in North America long ago?

Vocabulary

history

colony

settlers

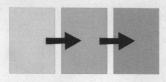

Sequence

Early America

History is the study of things that happened in the past. It tells about places and people and how they have changed over time.

The First North Americans

Native Americans were the first people to live in North America. Many different groups lived all over the continent. They knew how to find and grow food. They hunted animals for food and used the skins for clothing. Some communities built shelters from wood, while others used earth.

Farming in fields

A Native American tribe called the Powhatan used small trees to build their homes. First, they bent the trees and tied them together. Then they covered the trees with big pieces of tree bark. The people cooked on fires inside their homes.

Reading Check **Who were the first people in North America?**

A Powhatan Community

Hunting animals for food

Houses built from small trees and bark

Wall for protection

Making a dugout canoe

Colonies and Settlers

After a while, Native Americans were no longer the only people in North America. People from Europe decided to start colonies here. A **colony** is a place that is ruled by another country.

The European countries wanted to use the resources of North America. **Settlers** began traveling across the ocean to make new homes in North America.

Coming to North America

England

Plymouth
Jamestown

Atlantic Ocean

Map Key
Route to Plymouth
Route to Jamestown

 MAP SKILL Is Jamestown to the north or south of Plymouth?

The European country called England set up colonies along the Atlantic Ocean. The first was in what is now Virginia. A group of settlers built a colony called Jamestown. Then a group known as the Pilgrims settled in what is now Massachusetts. They began a colony called Plymouth. Soon England had thirteen colonies.

Reading Check **Focus Skill** **Sequence Which community was settled first, Plymouth or Jamestown?**

Help from the Native Americans

The settlers found that life was different from what they were used to. They had to build their own homes, grow their own food, and make their own furniture and clothing. Not everyone knew how to do this.

The Pilgrims and the Wampanoag had a feast together that has become known as Thanksgiving.

The settlers learned from the Native Americans where to hunt, fish, and gather food. They also learned how to grow new kinds of crops and build shelters. Native Americans helped the settlers survive in this new place.

Reading Check **How did Native Americans help the settlers?**

Summary Native Americans were the first people to live in North America. Settlers from other countries later started colonies here.

Review

1. **What to Know** What do we know about the people who lived in North America long ago?

2. **Vocabulary** How are Native Americans a part of America's **history**?

3. **Activity** Draw a picture that shows one way Native Americans helped the early North American settlers.

4. **Sequence** What happened after settlers arrived in North America?

183

Look at Native American History

You can learn how Native Americans lived long ago from primary sources. A **source** is the place something comes from.

DBQ ❶ What do these things tell us about Native American culture?

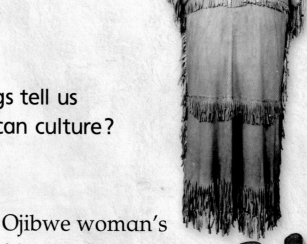

Ojibwe woman's clothing and moccasins

Haida mask

Cherokee cane basket

DBQ ② How did Native Americans use resources to meet their needs?

Zuni Pueblo water jar

Lenape shelter

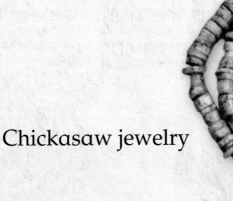

Chickasaw jewelry

✏ Write About It

What can primary sources tell you about history?

 For more resources, go to
www.harcourtschool.com/ss1

Independence

What to Know
How did our country get its independence?

Vocabulary
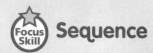
freedom

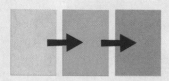
independence

Sequence

The people living in the thirteen English colonies had to obey the laws made by England's king. They thought that some of the king's laws were unfair.

King George III

The people of the colonies wanted the freedom to make their own laws. **Freedom** is the right of people to make their own choices.

"life, liberty, and the pursuit of happiness"

First Steps to Freedom

The leaders of the colonies decided to form their own country. First, they had a meeting. Then the Declaration of Independence was written. The leaders agreed to it on July 4, 1776.

Independence is the freedom of people to choose their own government. The Declaration of Independence said why the colonies should be free. It said that they were now states of a new country, the United States of America.

(Reading Check) **What happened on July 4, 1776?**

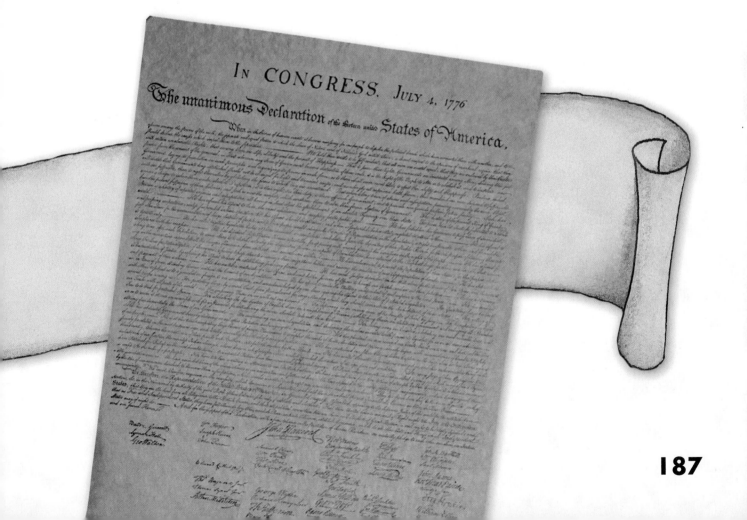

A War for Freedom

The king of England sent soldiers to fight against the people who wanted to be free. This war was called the American Revolution. Many brave people helped the colonies fight to become a free country.

Peter Salem helped win a battle in the war.

Women like Molly Pitcher helped win the war.

The war lasted for seven years. Finally, the colonies won. They were no longer ruled by England. The thirteen colonies were the first thirteen states of a free United States of America.

 **Reading Check** **Focus Skill** **Sequence**

What did the king of England do after he read the Declaration of Independence?

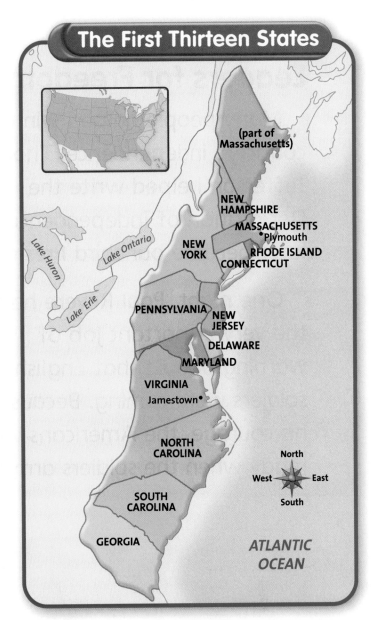

The First Thirteen States

(part of Massachusetts)

NEW HAMPSHIRE

MASSACHUSETTS
•Plymouth

NEW YORK

RHODE ISLAND

CONNECTICUT

Lake Huron

Lake Ontario

Lake Erie

PENNSYLVANIA

NEW JERSEY

DELAWARE

MARYLAND

VIRGINIA
Jamestown•

NORTH CAROLINA

North
West — East
South

SOUTH CAROLINA

GEORGIA

ATLANTIC OCEAN

MAP SKILL How many states did the United States have when it became a free country?

Leaders for Freedom

Many people helped win our country's independence. Thomas Jefferson helped write the Declaration of Independence. He later became our third President.

Thomas Jefferson

One night, Paul Revere had the very important job of warning people that English soldiers were coming. Because of his courage, the Americans were ready when the soldiers arrived.

Paul Revere

During the American Revolution, George Washington led the army. People trusted him because they knew he was a good leader. After the war, he became our country's first President.

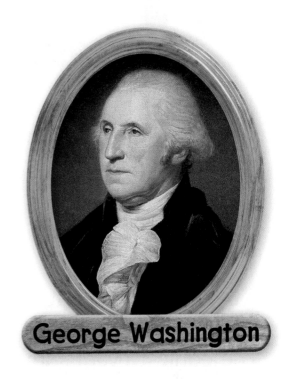

George Washington

Reading Check **Who was the first President of the United States?**

Summary People in the colonies fought a war for independence from England. They won, and the colonies became a free country.

Review

1. **What to Know** How did our country get its independence?

2. **Vocabulary** What is the Declaration of **Independence**?

3. **Write** Imagine that you are living in one of the new states. Tell about the events that led to independence in the order in which they happened.

4. **Sequence** Which came first, the Declaration of Independence or the end of the American Revolution?

Read a Time Line

Why It Matters   A **time line** shows important events in the order in which they happened.

Learn

You read a time line from left to right. The earliest events are on the left. A time line can show a long time or a short time. This one shows 15 years.

1775

1780

1776 The Declaration of Independence is written.

1781 The last big battle of the American Revolution is fought.

Practice

1 When was the last big battle of the war?

2 Did George Washington become President before or after the Declaration of Independence was written?

Apply

Make It Relevant Make a time line of important events in the history of your school or community.

For online activities, go to
www.harcourtschool.com/ss1

1785

1790

1789 George Washington becomes the first President.

Getting Others to Vote

Long ago, citizens of our country worked hard to get their own government and freedoms. Today, it is important to use our freedom to vote by taking part in elections.

When you turn 18 years old, you will be able to vote in elections. However, many people do not take the time to vote. A group called "Take Your Kids to Vote" wants families to learn about voting together. They think children will be more likely to vote when they are older if they see their parents vote first.

This boy watches as his father uses a voting machine.

194

Long ago, our country's leaders stood up for what they believed in. Today, people can help make changes in our country by voting. "Take Your Kids to Vote" has activities and ideas for parents and children. These help children know they can make a difference by voting when they are older.

Make It Relevant Why is it important for families to talk about voting?

Good citizens make every vote count!

195

American Heritage

What to Know
How do we honor our American heritage?

Vocabulary

heritage

landmark

memorial

 **Sequence**

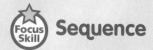

Symbols of Our Country

The bald eagle is a symbol of our heritage. Heritage is the traditions and values passed on by the people who lived before us. Our national bird reminds us of our freedom.

The stars and stripes on our flag are symbols, too. They stand for the people of the colonies who worked together to form the United States.

196

The Constitution was written when our government was formed. It lists the rights of all citizens. It is a symbol that reminds us of our freedoms.

The Statue of Liberty is a symbol of freedom for people who come to our country. It is a symbol that is also a landmark. A landmark is a feature that makes a location special.

The Statue of Liberty

Visitors can see the Constitution in Washington, D.C.

Reading Check **What are some of the symbols of our heritage?**

Memorials and Monuments

Some symbols of our country are also memorials. A memorial is something people create to remember a person or an event. When we look at the Washington Monument, we remember George Washington and all that he did for our country. The Jefferson Memorial honors Thomas Jefferson, who helped write the Declaration of Independence.

The Washington Monument

The Jefferson Memorial

The Lincoln Memorial honors President Abraham Lincoln. He kept our country together during the Civil War. This was a time when Americans fought one another.

The Lincoln Memorial

Reading Check **What symbol honors George Washington?**

Summary Symbols, landmarks, and memorials remind us of our American heritage.

Review

① **What to Know** How do we honor our American heritage?

② **Vocabulary** Why do you think it is important to remember our **heritage**?

③ **Activity** Draw a picture of a landmark or memorial you know about. Write a sentence to tell who or what it honors and why.

④ **Sequence** What did President Lincoln do before the Lincoln Memorial was built?

💡 **What to Know**
How do we honor people and events in our country's history?

Vocabulary

hero

legend

⭐ **Sequence**
Focus Skill

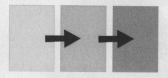

Heroes and Holidays

Heroes make a difference in people's lives with their actions. A **hero** is a person who has done something brave or important.

Heroes in History

Harriet Tubman and Sojourner Truth were heroes when African Americans had few or no rights. Both worked for equal rights for women and African Americans.

Harriet Tubman

Sojourner Truth

Some heroes are alive today. Neil Armstrong was the first person to walk on the moon. He is a hero because he explored space for our country.

Some heroes come from legends. A legend is a story passed down through history. The people in legends are heroes, but many of their actions are made up. John Henry, Johnny Appleseed, Betsy Ross, and Paul Bunyan are heroes from legends. The stories about them are part of our country's heritage.

The Story of
JOHNNY APPLESEED
Written and illustrated by Aliki

Aladdin Paperbacks

BETSY ROSS
written and illustrated by
Alexandra Wallner

Holiday House, Inc.

Reading Check Who is a hero that is still alive today?

Holidays and Celebrations

The United States has many holidays, or days on which we celebrate or remember something. Some holidays help us remember our country's heroes. Other holidays help us remember important events.

The third Monday in February is a holiday called Presidents' Day. Both George Washington and Abraham Lincoln were born in February. This holiday honors all the Presidents who have served our country.

We celebrate Memorial Day at the end of May. On this day we honor the men and women who gave their lives for our country.

The first Monday in September is Labor Day. Labor is work. On Labor Day, we honor all of the people who work in our country. Many people celebrate this day by spending time with their families.

Independence Day is also known as the Fourth of July. On July 4, 1776, leaders of the thirteen colonies agreed to the Declaration of Independence. Communities celebrate this day with parades, speeches, and fireworks.

Reading Check **Focus Skill** **Sequence** Which comes first during the year, Labor Day or Presidents' Day?

The Centennial Celebration

On July 4, 1876, our country was 100 years old. Seventeen-year-old Frank L. Thomas from New Jersey visited the Centennial Exhibition in Philadelphia, Pennsylvania. Frank kept a journal about what he saw. More than nine million visitors came to see what our country had done in its first hundred years.

A page from Frank's journal

Summary We honor people and events in history by having holidays to remember them.

Review

1. **What to Know** How do we honor people and events in our country's history?

2. **Vocabulary** What kind of story is a **legend**?

3. **Activity** Choose an American that you would like to honor with a special holiday. Draw a picture that shows how this holiday would be celebrated. Add a caption that explains your picture.

4. **Sequence** Which holiday do we celebrate on the first Monday in September?

Tell Fact from Fiction

Why It Matters You need to be able to tell if what you read is true.

Learn

1 A **fact** is a statement that can be proved true. **Nonfiction** books have only facts.

2 **Fiction** stories may seem real, but some of the information is made up.

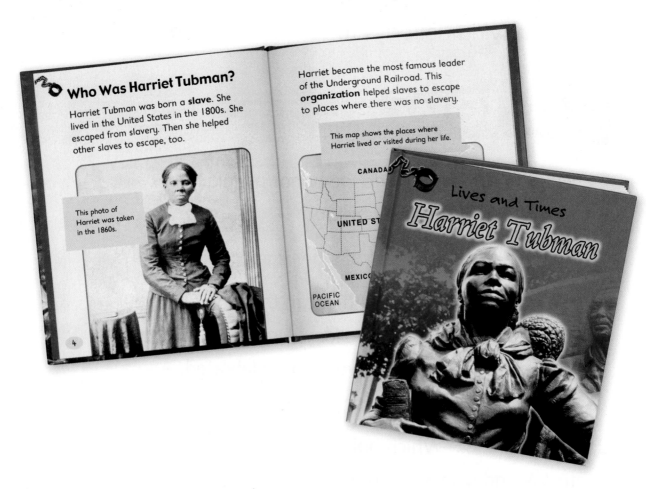

Who Was Harriet Tubman?

Harriet Tubman was born a **slave**. She lived in the United States in the 1800s. She escaped from slavery. Then she helped other slaves to escape, too.

This photo of Harriet was taken in the 1860s.

Harriet became the most famous leader of the Underground Railroad. This **organization** helped slaves to escape to places where there was no slavery.

This map shows the places where Harriet lived or visited during her life.

CANADA

UNITED ST

MEXICO

PACIFIC OCEAN

Lives and Times
Harriet Tubman

Practice

Look at the two books. Decide which one is fact and which one is fiction.

Apply

Make It Relevant Find a book in your library about a hero you would like to know more about. Will the book be fact or fiction?

Biography

Trustworthiness

Respect

Responsibility

Fairness

Caring

Patriotism

Dr. Martin Luther King, Jr.

Why Character Counts

How did Dr. Martin Luther King, Jr., show responsibility?

Growing up, Martin Luther King, Jr., was not allowed to eat at certain restaurants. He also had to sit at the back of a bus. This was because of the color of his skin. Martin Luther King, Jr., took the responsibility of leading people to change these rules.

Dr. Martin Luther King, Jr., worked for equal rights.

Dr. King led many people in the fight for equal rights for African Americans.

It was important to Dr. King to find peaceful ways to solve problems. He led marches to spread his message. Dr. King said, "Our lives begin to end the day we become silent about things that matter."

Dr. King was a hero whose work made a difference in our country. In 1964, a new law was made. It said that people cannot be separated or given fewer rights because of the color of their skin. Today, Dr. Martin Luther King, Jr., is honored on a national holiday in January.

GO ONLINE For more resources, go to **www.harcourtschool.com/ss1**

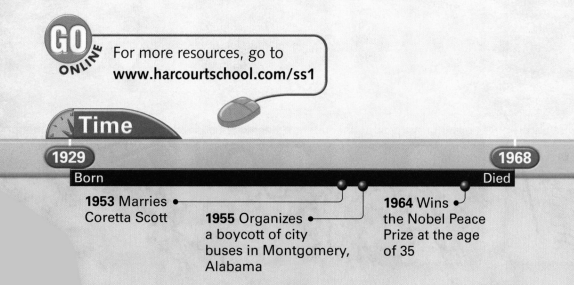

Time

1929			1968
Born			Died

1953 Marries Coretta Scott

1955 Organizes a boycott of city buses in Montgomery, Alabama

1964 Wins the Nobel Peace Prize at the age of 35

Holiday Mix-Up

Find the picture that does not belong in each row.

Word Fun

Answer the questions.

Which letter do the words past, present, and future have in common?

Which letter of the alphabet can replace the h in hero and turn it into a number?

What does a table have that is in the word legend?

Answer the riddle.

Where do both settlers and ants live?

Online Adventures

GO ONLINE

Join Eco on a trip to a history museum. You will go on a roller coaster ride through the past and the present. Play now, at www.harcourtschool.com/ss1

Review and Test Prep

The Big Idea

History History is the story of how people and places change over time.

Sequence

(Focus Skill)

Copy and fill in the chart to show what you have learned about the history of our country's independence.

First

The leaders of the colonies decided to form their own country and had a meeting.

Next

_____
_____

Last

_____
_____

✓ Vocabulary

Match the word to its meaning.

1. the freedom of people to choose their own government

2. a feature that makes a location special

3. what happens when something becomes different

4. the study of things in the past

5. a place that is ruled by another country

Word Bank

change
(p. 174)

history
(p. 178)

colony
(p. 180)

independence
(p. 187)

landmark
(p. 197)

✓ Facts and Main Ideas

6. How do communities change over time?

7. Who were the first people to live in North America?

8. How did Thomas Jefferson help our country?

9. Which of these shows important events in the order in which they happened?

   A picture graph   **C** family tree

   B diagram   **D** time line

10. Which holiday honors people who gave their lives for our country?

    A Presidents' Day   **C** Memorial Day

    B Labor Day   **D** Independence Day

⑪ How does learning about the past help us in the future?

⑫ **Make It Relevant** How has learning about people in history made a difference in your life?

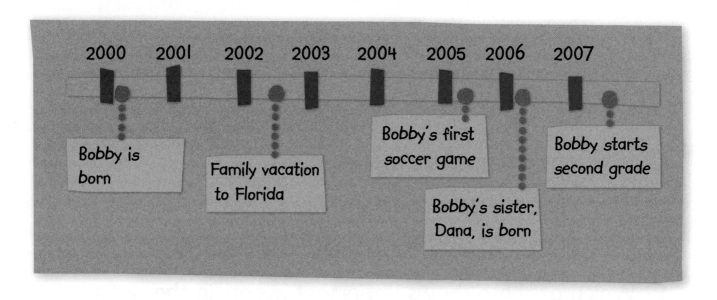

⑬ In what year was Bobby born?

⑭ When was Bobby's first soccer game?

⑮ Was Dana born before or after the family vacation?

⑯ When did Bobby start second grade?

Simon & Schuster Books for Young Readers

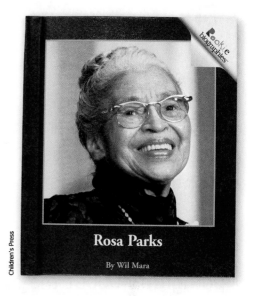

Children's Press

⑰ Which book do you think is fiction?

⑱ What clues lead you to believe that it is fiction?

⑲ What is the title of the nonfiction book?

⑳ Which book do you think would have more facts about Rosa Parks? Why?

Activities

Show What You Know

Unit Writing Activity

All About You Think about your past and present. What events do you want to share?

Write a Narrative Paragraph Write a paragraph about the events. Put them in sequence.

Unit Project

Historical Journal Create a journal with entries by people in history.

- Pick a person and write a journal entry from his or her point of view.
- Put the entries in order.

Read More

The Pledge of Allegiance: Symbols of Freedom
by Lola Schaefer

If You Were at the First Thanksgiving
by Anne Kamma

Judy Moody Declares Independence
by Megan McDonald

GO ONLINE

For more resources, go to www.harcourtschool.com/ss1

Long Ago and Today

The first communities in Indiana were Native American villages. Some early tribes in Indiana were the Miami, Potawatomi, and Lenape. These groups farmed, hunted, and fished.

The Lenape Indians lived in villages near rivers.

What to Know 💡
How have Indiana communities changed over time?

Vocabulary
explorer
   p. IN 4-2
founded
   p. IN 4-4
skyscraper
   p. IN 4-6

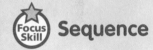
Focus Skill **Sequence**

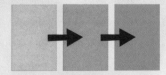

Explorers and Settlers

Later, explorers from France claimed land in North America. Indiana was part of that land. An **explorer** is a person who goes to find out about a place.

The French began to trade with the Native Americans. The settlers built trading posts, which became small communities. One of these posts was called Vincennes. Later, more settlers moved west from the English colonies to Indiana.

Reading Check **Focus Skill** **Sequence**

Who were the first people to live in Indiana?

Early Vincennes

Vincennes Today

Starting New Communities

Hoosiers built communities for many reasons. Some communities began as forts or trading posts. Others were started because of location. For example, some communities began near a river or a main road.

Indianapolis was started in the early 1800s because of its location. Hoosiers wanted a new capital located in the middle of the state. Indianapolis is still the state capital.

MAP SKILL In what part of the state is Indianapolis?

Reading Check Why was Indianapolis started?

Early Indianapolis

Indianapolis Today

New Albany was founded by three brothers from New York.

People and Communities

Communities in Indiana started at different times. Many large cities began more than 100 years ago. These communities were started, or **founded**, by one person or by a group. Some communities are named for famous people.

Reading Check For whom was Clarksville named?

Jeffersonville was named for Thomas Jefferson.

Clarksville honors George Rogers Clark.

Communities Grow

Many communities start small and grow over time. The city of Marion began as a small town. It was started in 1831 along the Mississinewa River.

Later, natural gas was found nearby. Hoosiers could use the gas as fuel for making glass and other goods. Many businesses were started, and Marion grew quickly.

Reading Check **What made Marion grow quickly?**

Natural gas caused many Indiana communities to grow.

Marion grew out of a small farming community.

Communities Change

The way communities look changes over time. At first, Fort Wayne had small buildings made of wood, stone, or brick. Today, it has **skyscrapers**, or very tall buildings. Skyscrapers are made of steel and glass.

Daily life in a community changes, too. Hoosiers long ago did not have electricity, telephones, or computers. Children learned at home or in small one-room schools. They read their lessons aloud. They also helped their teacher do chores.

Reading Check **How do communities change over time?**

One-Room Schoolhouse

A School Today

Who Helped Your Community Grow?

People and businesses help communities grow. The Studebaker brothers lived in South Bend. They began making cars in the early 1900s. Their company helped South Bend grow. This new kind of transportation also helped other cities grow.

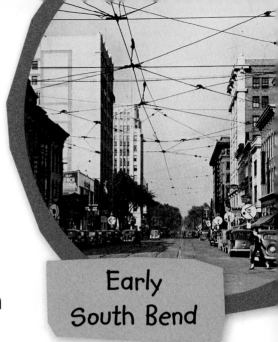

Early South Bend

Your community also has a story. Who founded your community? What made your community grow?

Reading Check **Who helped South Bend grow?**

Studebaker Brothers

Studebaker Car

Community Celebrations

December 11 is Statehood Day, or Indiana Day. On that day in 1816, Indiana became the nineteenth state.

Some communities celebrate by honoring a founder. Others have Pioneer Days.

Reading Check **What is Statehood Day in Indiana?**

Indiana Day Celebration

Summary Indiana communities were founded at different times and for different reasons. Life in Indiana has changed over time.

Review

1. **What to Know** How have Indiana communities changed over time?

2. **Vocabulary** Where is a **skyscraper** in Indiana?

3. ✏️ **Write** Do research to learn how your community began. Write how your community has changed.

4. 🌟 **Sequence** Who were the first people to meet Native Americans in Indiana?

A World of Many People

Start with the Standards

Indiana's Academic Standards for Social Studies

History 2.1.3, 2.1.4, 2.1.6

Civics and Government 2.2.4, 2.2.5, 2.2.7

The Big Idea

Culture
Our country is made up of many different people and cultures.

What to Know

✔ What is culture?

✔ Why is the United States a country of many cultures?

✔ How are families different? How are they alike?

✔ Who are some Americans who have made a difference in our lives?

Festivals in Indiana

Hoosiers take part in festivals that honor their cultures. A festival is a gathering for celebration. Some festivals celebrate cultures in Indiana. These festivals help Hoosiers think about where their families came from.

In Jasper, Hoosiers take part in Strassenfest. This festival celebrates Indiana's German culture. Many people in Indiana have family members who came from Germany.

In the summer, Hoosiers can go to the Indian Market in Indianapolis. There they can see Native American art. They also hear Native American music.

Every year, many Hoosiers go to the Fiesta Fort Wayne. This festival honors Hispanic culture with movies, dance, and food.

The yearly Indiana Festival celebrates the many cultures of Hoosiers. Visitors can see the different parts of these cultures, such as dances from Asian countries.

Indiana TEST PREP

① Which festival honors Native American art and music?

A Strassenfest

B Indian Market

C Taste of Asia

D Africana Festival

② At which festival can visitors learn about Indiana's many cultures?

A Indian Market

B Fiesta Fort Wayne

C Indiana Festival

D Strassenfest

③ **Writing** What cultural festivals are celebrated in your community?

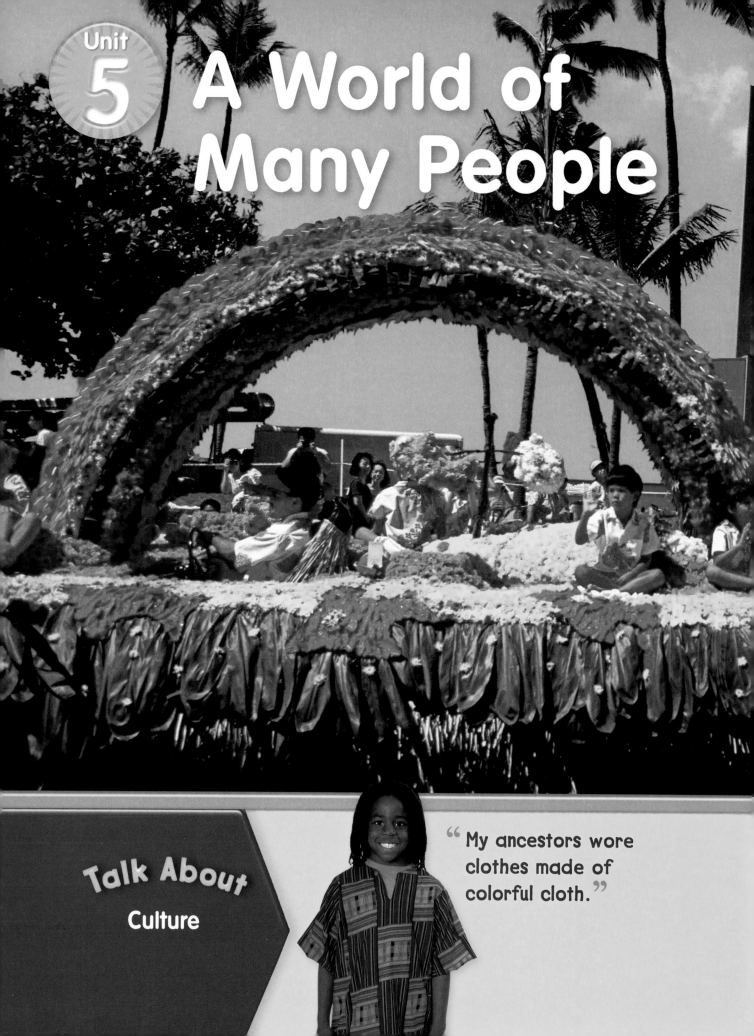

A World of Many People

Talk About
Culture

"My ancestors wore clothes made of colorful cloth."

" Aloha! I welcome friends with leis. "

" Hola means hello in Spanish. "

Vocabulary

culture   A group's way of life.

(page 226)

immigrant   Someone who comes from another place to live in a country.

(page 236)

custom A group's way of doing something. (page 246)

tradition Something that is passed on from older family members to children. (page 246)

GO ONLINE For more resources, go to www.harcourtschool.com/ss1

Reading Social Studies

Recall and Retell

Why It Matters It is important to remember and understand what you read.

Learn

As you read, be sure to recall and retell information.

● To recall, think about what you have just read.

● To retell, put that information in your own words.

Read the paragraph below.

Recall St. Lucia Day is a Swedish holiday. It is celebrated on December 13 because it is one of the shortest days of the year. Girls dress in white robes with red or white sashes. They wear wreaths with candles on their heads. Boys carry poles with stars on the tops. Everyone eats sweet buns and pinwheel cookies.

Practice

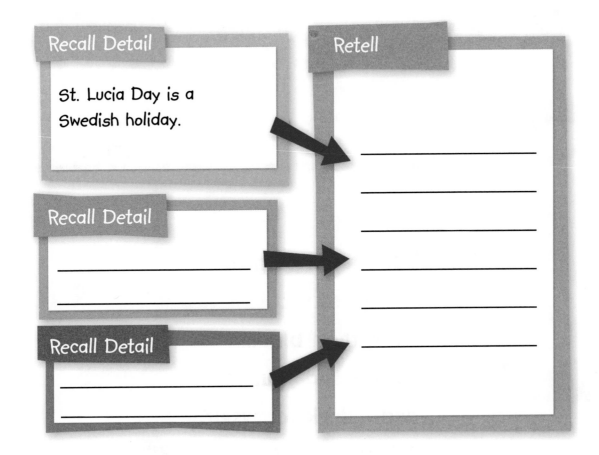

Recall Detail

St. Lucia Day is a Swedish holiday.

Recall Detail

_____

_____

Recall Detail

_____

_____

Retell

_____

_____

_____

_____

_____

_____

_____

Copy the chart and complete it. Write details you recall from what you just read. Then use your own words to retell what you read.

Apply

As you read, recall and retell information about people in this unit.

What a Wonderful World

by George David Weiss and Bob Thiele

illustrated by Ashley Bryan

I see trees of green,

red roses too,

I see them bloom

for me and you,

and I think to myself,

"What a wonderful world!"

I see skies of blue
and clouds of white,
the bright, blessed day,
the dark, sacred night,
and I think to myself,
"What a wonderful world!"

The colors of the rainbow, so pretty in the sky
are also on the faces of people going by.
I see friends shaking hands, saying, "How do you do?"
They're really saying, "I love you."

I hear babies cry, I watch them grow.
They'll learn much more than I'll ever know,
and I think to myself,
"What a wonderful world!"
Yes, I think to myself,
"What a wonderful world!"

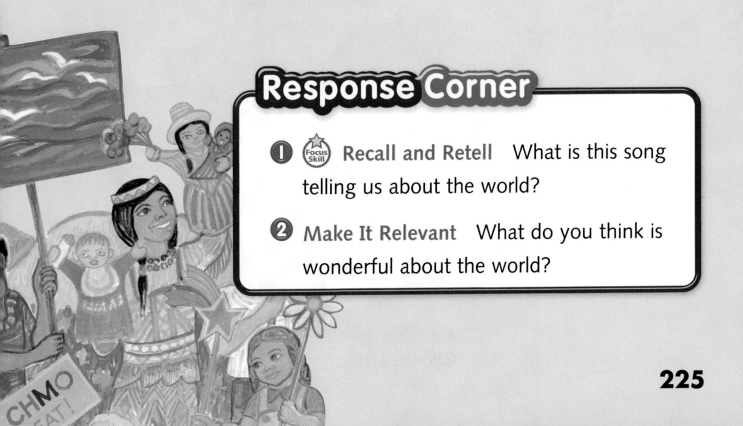

Response Corner

❶ (Focus Skill) **Recall and Retell** What is this song telling us about the world?

❷ **Make It Relevant** What do you think is wonderful about the world?

225

Lesson 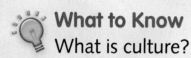 1

💡 **What to Know**
What is culture?

Vocabulary
culture
language

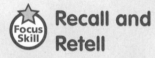 **Recall and Retell**

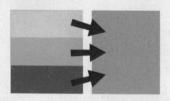

World Cultures

Our world is made up of many cultures. **Culture** is a group's way of life. Food, clothes, art, music, and beliefs are all parts of a group's culture.

A Community in Ghana

Abena lives in Ghana, a country in Africa. The people in her village sell fruits, vegetables, and crafts at the market.

A market in Ghana, Africa

Besides English, people in Abena's village speak a **language** called Twi. The children listen to folktales told in Twi. Many of the stories are about Anansi the spider. The people of Ghana say that it was Anansi who brought stories to the world.

A folktale from Ghana

Reading Check **Recall and Retell** **What things are parts of Abena's culture?**

A Community in Spain

Eduardo lives with his family in Cordoba, a city in Spain. Eating together is an important part of family life in Spain. The biggest meal of the day is lunch. Many businesses close then so that people can go home to eat with their families.

Paella, a rice dish, is a favorite meal in Spain.

Cordoba, Spain

Every year during the last week of May, Cordoba holds a big festival. The streets fill with people who come to see the parade of horses, the lights, and dancing to guitar music.

Reading Check **What is an important part of Spanish family life?**

Flamenco dancer

A Community in Japan

Yukio lives in Aomori, Japan. Many people in Japan eat with chopsticks. They sit on cushions on the floor at a low table. Favorite foods are rice, seaweed, vegetables with meat, and raw fish called sushi.

The Nebuta Festival in Aomori celebrates summer with a parade of colorful floats. Everyone takes part and dances to the drums and bamboo flutes.

Reading Check **What do people eat with in Japan?**

Aomori, Japan

230

Aomori's Nebuta Festival

Summary People in countries around the world have different cultures.

Review

1. **What to Know** What is culture?

2. **Vocabulary** What **language** do you speak as part of your culture?

3. ✏️ **Write** Choose a culture in your community. Write a short paragraph about things that are part of this culture.

4. ⭐(Focus Skill) **Recall and Retell** Who do people in Ghana say brought stories to the world?

Find Locations on a World Map

Why It Matters   We can use a world map to find countries and their neighbors.

Learn

❶ There are more than 190 countries in the world. Russia is the largest country. China has the most people.

❷ Countries that are close together are more alike than different.

Practice

❶ Which continent has more countries, South America or Africa?

❷ Which continent is Japan a part of?

❸ Which countries are Spain's neighbors?

The World

ARCTIC OCEAN

ICELAND
NORWAY FINLAND
SWEDEN
UNITED
KINGDOM BELARUS
POLAND
GERMANY UKRAINE
FRANCE
SPAIN ITALY
GREECE ROMANIA
TURKEY
MOROCCO TUNISIA
ALGERIA LIBYA EGYPT
MAURITANIA
MALI NIGER SUDAN
CHAD
NIGERIA
ETHIOPIA
SOMALIA
GHANA
CAMEROON UGANDA
GABON DEM. KENYA
REP. REP. CONGO CONGO TANZANIA
ANGOLA
ZAMBIA MOZAMBIQUE
MADAGASCAR
BOTSWANA ZIMBABWE
NAMIBIA
SWAZILAND
SOUTH LESOTHO
AFRICA

RUSSIA

KAZAKHSTAN MONGOLIA

JAPAN
CHINA

SOUTH
KOREA
TAIWAN

AFGHANISTAN

IRAQ IRAN
PAKISTAN
SAUDI
ARABIA OMAN INDIA
YEMEN
THAILAND LAOS PHILIPPINES
VIETNAM
CAMBODIA
MALAYSIA
SRI
LANKA

INDONESIA
PAPUA
NEW GUINEA

FIJI

PACIFIC
OCEAN

INDIAN
OCEAN

AUSTRALIA

NEW
ZEALAND

ATLANTIC
OCEAN

SOUTHERN OCEAN

North
West East
South

Map Key
North America
South America
Europe
Africa
Asia
Australia
Antarctica

Apply

Make It Relevant   Name the country or countries your family came from. Find them on a world map or a globe.

GO ONLINE   For online activities, go to
www.harcourtschool.com/ss1

Learning About Cultures

People all over the world express their culture in different ways. Some people show it through their clothing, while others express it through music, pottery, and many other kinds of art.

DBQ ❶ What do these things show about a culture?

Mask from
Colombia

Maracas from
Mexico

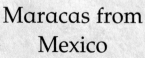

Kimono from
Japan

DBQ ② How can you use these things to compare cultures?

Hat from Peru

Mud cloth from Mali

Boots from Turkey

 Write About It

How are the things on these pages like things from your culture?

GO ONLINE For more resources, go to www.harcourtschool.com/ss1

What to Know
Why is the United States a country of many cultures?

Vocabulary
immigrant
diversity

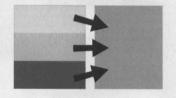
Recall and Retell

Many People, One Country

On a city street, you may see a Chinese, French, or Italian restaurant. You may hear people speaking Spanish, Arabic, and other languages. Immigrants have brought their cultures to the United States. An **immigrant** is someone who comes from another place to live in a country.

These immigrants are taking part in a ceremony to become American citizens.

Coming to the United States

Immigrants have been coming to the United States for many years and for many different reasons. In the past, immigrants from Ireland came because they did not have enough food. Today, immigrants from some African countries come to escape war. Many immigrants come to the United States for a better life.

Reading Check **What is a reason immigrants come to the United States?**

Many immigrants who came in the past arrived at Ellis Island in New York Harbor.

Cultural Differences

At first, life in a new country is hard. Immigrants have to find new homes and new jobs. They may have to learn a new language and new ways of doing things.

As immigrants learn about the culture of their new country, they also keep their own culture. They pass on their old ways of doing things to their children and grandchildren.

People in this community keep up their Chinese language and culture.

Dhanya's parents are from India. Her father plays Indian songs on a sitar, a stringed instrument. For many Indian celebrations, Dhanya wears a colorful dress called a sari.

Anthony's family loves to get together with neighbors to play bocce ball. Bocce ball is a game that is played in Italy. Anthony's grandfather taught him how to play.

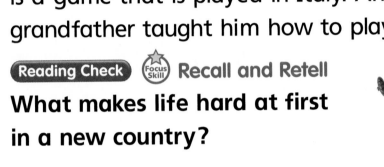

Reading Check **Focus Skill** **Recall and Retell**

What makes life hard at first in a new country?

Diversity in America Today

Immigrants bring **diversity**, or many different ideas and ways of living. We see this in our many kinds of food, clothing, music, dance, languages, and beliefs. Because cultures have different ideas and beliefs, people in our country have many different points of view. We learn from each other's ideas and share different ways of living.

We come from different cultures, but we are all Americans. We share a belief in freedom and the rights of every citizen.

Reading Check **What are some kinds of diversity in the United States?**

Summary Immigrants from other countries and cultures bring diversity to the United States.

Review

① **What to Know** Why is the United States a country of many cultures?

② **Vocabulary** Name some **immigrant** groups who have come to the United States.

③ **Activity** Interview family members about how and why your family came to the United States.

④ **Recall and Retell** How do immigrants change the United States?

Working Together

Why It Matters Sometimes when people work in a group, there is conflict. **Conflict** happens when people have different points of view on what to do or how to do it. To get a job done, people must cooperate, or work together.

Learn

Following these steps will help members of a group cooperate to get a job done.

❶ Listen to each person's ideas. Plan together how to do the job.

❷ Give each person a task.

❸ When the job is done, talk about it.

Practice

Suppose your group wants to make a bulletin board showing different cultures in your school. Work together to list the steps. Write what to do in each step.

Apply

Make It Relevant Work together in a group to research a culture in your community or state.

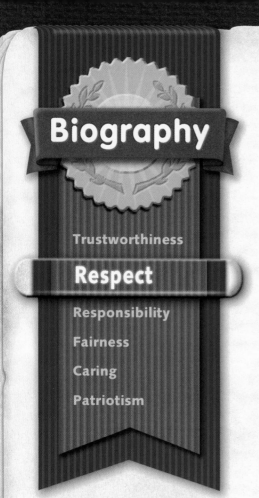

Trustworthiness

Respect

Responsibility

Fairness

Caring

Patriotism

Why Character Counts

✎ How does Amy Tan show respect for her culture?

Amy Tan

Amy Tan was born in Oakland, California, but her parents were born in China. In the 1940s, they left China to find a safer place to live. They moved to the United States.

When Amy Tan was young, she used her imagination to write. When she was eight years old, she won first prize for an essay she wrote. It was called "What the Library Means to Me."

Amy Tan is an Asian American author.

Amy Tan's stories tell about her family's history.

Amy Tan now writes stories about her family. She is an American who remembers the Chinese traditions of her family's past. She uses her writing as a way to honor her family's history.

In her stories for children, Amy Tan shares her Chinese heritage.

GO **ONLINE** For more resources, go to www.harcourtschool.com/ss1

Time

| 1952 | | | Present |

Born

1969 Finishes high school in Switzerland

1985 Takes a writing class that leads to her first book

1989 Publishes her first book, The Joy Luck Club

Celebrating Culture

💡 **What to Know**
How are families different? How are they alike?

Vocabulary
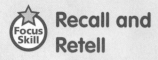
custom
tradition

Focus Skill **Recall and Retell**

Families in the United States celebrate their cultures. They may do different things, but families are alike in many ways.

David's Family

David and his family are Jewish. They have **customs**, or ways of doing things. They also have traditions. A **tradition** is something that is passed from older family members to children.

My family celebrating Shabbat

Every Friday night, it is a tradition for all of David's family to share a special meal for Shabbat. They know that many Jewish families all over the world are sharing this tradition.

David's parents want their children to do well in school. David and his sister also go to a Jewish school to learn about Jewish customs and traditions. They are also learning the Hebrew language.

Reading Check **What do Jewish people all over the world share?**

My sister studying Hebrew

My older brother's bar mitzvah

247

Luz's Family

Luz and her family are Mexican American. They speak both Spanish and English. It is a custom to celebrate birthdays with big parties. They also celebrate holidays, such as Easter. It is a family tradition to celebrate these holidays at Luz's grandparents' house.

Luz's parents were not able to go to college in Mexico. They want their children to study hard, go to college, and get good jobs.

Reading Check **Why do Luz's parents want their children to study hard?**

When my sister turned fifteen years old, she had a big party called a Quinceañera.

Easter celebration at my grandmother's house

David's Family

Jewish American

Shares Shabbat

Children learn
Hebrew

Both

Value education

Spend time together

Luz's Family

Mexican Amercian

Celebrates Easter

Speaks Spanish
and English

How are the customs of these two cultures alike?

Summary Families of different cultures have special customs and traditions.

Review

1. **What to Know** How are families different? How are they alike?

2. **Vocabulary** How is a **tradition** different from other activities?

3. **Activity** Make a storyboard of pictures showing customs and traditions your family celebrates. Add captions to your pictures.

4. **Recall and Retell** What is a tradition both families had in this lesson?

249

Read a Calendar

Why It Matters   A **calendar** is a chart that keeps track of the days in a week, month, or year. You can use a calendar to measure time or to find special days.

Learn

❶ There are seven days in a week.

❷ There are about four weeks in a month. Most months have 30 or 31 days. February has just 28 days or, in some years, 29 days.

❸ There are 12 months in a year.

Practice

❶ How many days are in this month?

❷ What special day is Sunday, March 25?

❸ When is St. Patrick's Day?

March

Sunday	Monday	Tuesday	Wednesday	Thursday	Friday	Saturday
				1	2	3
4	5	6 School Red, White and Blue Day	7	8	9	10
11	12	13	14	15	16	17 St. Patrick's Day
18	19	20	21	22 India's New Year's Day	23	24 Annual Town Spring Festival
25 Greek Independence Day	26	27	28	29	30	31

Apply

Make It Relevant Make a calendar page for next month. Show events that will happen at school and in your community.

GO ONLINE For online activities, go to
www.harcourtschool.com/ss1

Field Trip

Read About

Every July, the Grandfather Mountain Highland Games in North Carolina honor the culture of people from Scotland. At the games, you can see traditional Scottish clothing, such as kilts and tartan plaids. You can watch Scottish games and dancing, listen to music, and eat Scottish foods. You can also learn about the history of many families who came to the United States from Scotland.

Find

United States

Linville, North Carolina

Grandfather Mountain Highland Games

Caber toss

Parade of the Tartans

Bagpipe musicians

Highland dancer

Sheepherding contest

A Virtual Tour

GO ONLINE For more resources, go to
www.harcourtschool.com/ss1

Recognizing Americans

What to Know
Who are some Americans who have made a difference in our lives?

Vocabulary

scientist

invention

Recall and Retell

Many different people live in the United States. Some Americans have done important things that have affected our lives and culture.

Famous Scientists

Thomas Edison was a **scientist**, a person who observes things and makes discoveries. His most famous invention was the lightbulb. An **invention** is a new product that has not been made before.

" Genius is one percent inspiration, ninety-nine percent perspiration. "

Thomas Edison

George Washington Carver was a scientist who helped farmers. He showed that growing peanuts, soybeans, and sweet potatoes made poor soil rich again. He also found new ways to use these crops. They could be used to make medicines and even glue.

Reading Check **Focus Skill** **Recall and Retell** **In what ways did Edison and Carver improve people's lives?**

"Where there is no vision, there is no hope."

George Washington Carver

Fast Fact!

George Washington Carver found that more than 300 products could be made from peanuts. Some of these are peanut butter, ink, and shampoo.

Famous Artists

Ieoh Ming Pei is a Chinese American architect, or a person who designs buildings. He designs interesting buildings that become landmarks in urban areas in the United States and around the world.

"Take your position and have faith in yourself."

Ieoh Ming Pei

Rock and Roll Hall of Fame and Museum in Cleveland, Ohio

ELVIS IS IN THE BUILDING

ROCK AND ROLL HALL OF FAME AND MUSEUM
ONE KEY PLAZA

Gloria Estefan is a singer, dancer, and songwriter. Through her music, she shares her Cuban culture. Estefan's songs have helped make Latin music popular in the United States. She also holds concerts to raise money to help people in need.

Reading Check **How have Ieoh Ming Pei and Gloria Estefan affected American culture?**

Summary Some Americans have done important things that have made a difference in our lives.

"I strongly feel that we are all connected."

Gloria Estefan

Review

1. **What to Know** Who are some Americans who have made a difference in our lives?

2. **Vocabulary** What was Thomas Edison's most famous **invention**?

3. ✏ **Write** Write a paragraph about people in your community or state who have affected your life.

4. ⭐ **Recall and Retell** How does Gloria Estefan help other people?

Fun with Social Studies

Add Them Up

Match these people with the answers to the problems.

Gloria Estefan

George Washington Carver

Ieoh Ming Pei

Thomas Edison

258

Missing Letters

Use the missing letters to answer the riddle.

Word | **Clue**

l**?**ngu**?**ge | the words people use to communicate

i**?**ventio**?** | a new product that has not been made before

?radi**?**ion | something passed down from older family members to children

?cienti**?**t | a person who observes things and makes discoveries

What do uncles find at picnics?

? **?** **?** **?**

Online Adventures

GO ONLINE

A culture fair is coming to Eco's school. Visit the online fair to play games and learn about the cultures of many places. Play now, at www.harcourtschool.com/ss1

Review and Test Prep

 The Big Idea

Culture Our country is made up of many different people and cultures.

Recall and Retell

Copy and fill in the chart to recall and retell what you have learned about Americans who have done important things for our country.

Americans Who Made a Difference

Recall Detail

Scientists observe things and make discoveries.

Recall Detail

Recall Detail

Retell

Vocabulary

Test Prep

Choose the word that matches the description.

Word Bank

culture
  (p. 226)

immigrant
  (p. 236)

tradition
  (p. 246)

custom
  (p. 246)

1. Dhanya's father came here from India.

2. Anthony's family is Italian American.

3. Yukio eats with chopsticks.

4. Luz's parents pass down how their family celebrates special days.

Facts and Main Ideas

Test Prep

5. What are parts of a group's culture?

6. What is an immigrant?

7. What beliefs do many Americans share?

8. What can happen when people have different points of view?

9. Which word describes the many ideas and ways of living we find in the United States?

    A immigrant
    B language
    C diversity
    D tradition

10. Which American helped farmers grow crops?

    A George Washington Carver
    B Gloria Estefan
    C Ieoh Ming Pei
    D Thomas Edison

Critical Thinking

⑪ How would life be different today if Thomas Edison had not invented the electric lightbulb?

⑫ **Make It Relevant** How do customs and traditions make your family special?

Skills

September

Sunday	Monday	Tuesday	Wednesday	Thursday	Friday	Saturday
						1
2	3 Labor Day	4	5	6	7	8
9 Grandparent's Day	10	11	12	13	14	15
16	17	18	19	20	21	22 Yom Kippur
23 First Day of Autumn 30	24	25	26	27	28 Native American Day	29

⑬ How many days are in this month?

⑭ What special day is Friday, September 28?

⑮ When is Grandparents' Day?

⑯ What happens on September 23?

Countries in the East

Map Key
Europe
Africa
Asia
Australia

⑰ Which continent has more countries, Africa or Australia?

⑱ On which continent is Pakistan located?

⑲ Which countries are Egypt's neighbors?

⑳ Which ocean is north of Finland?

Activities

Show What You Know

 Unit Writing Activity

Remember Traditions Think about a tradition in your family. Why do you have it?

Write a Diary Entry Write a diary entry about a day you celebrate a tradition.

 Unit Project

Storyboard Design a family history storyboard.

- Interview family members.
- Collect photographs or draw pictures of events.
- Put the pictures in order.
- Share your storyboard.

Read More

Lee & Low Books, Inc.

Goldfish and Chrysanthemums by Michelle Cheng

Phyllis Fogelman Books

The Color of Home by Mary Hoffman

Salish Kootenai College Press

How Marten Got His Spots and Other Kootenai Indian Stories by Kootenai Cultural Committee

 For more resources, go to **www.harcourtschool.com/ss1**

People in the Marketplace

Unit
6

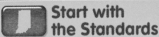

The Big Idea

Work

Producers and consumers depend on each other for goods and services.

What to Know

✔ How do producers and consumers depend on each other?

✔ How do people get money to pay for goods and services?

✔ How do raw materials become products?

✔ Why do we make, sell, and buy more of some things than others?

✔ How does trade help people meet their needs?

Jobs in Indiana

Did You Know?

The Indianapolis Motor Speedway was built so that carmakers could test their cars.

People in Indiana have different kinds of jobs. Some people work to make goods. Others provide services for their community.

Some workers in Indiana make car parts. School buses and fire engines are also made in the state. Workers make the car parts with steel from Indiana steel mills.

Farmers in Indiana grow food. Many of these farmers grow corn and soybeans. This food is sold in Indiana and across the country. Some farmers in Indiana raise animals, such as cattle and pigs.

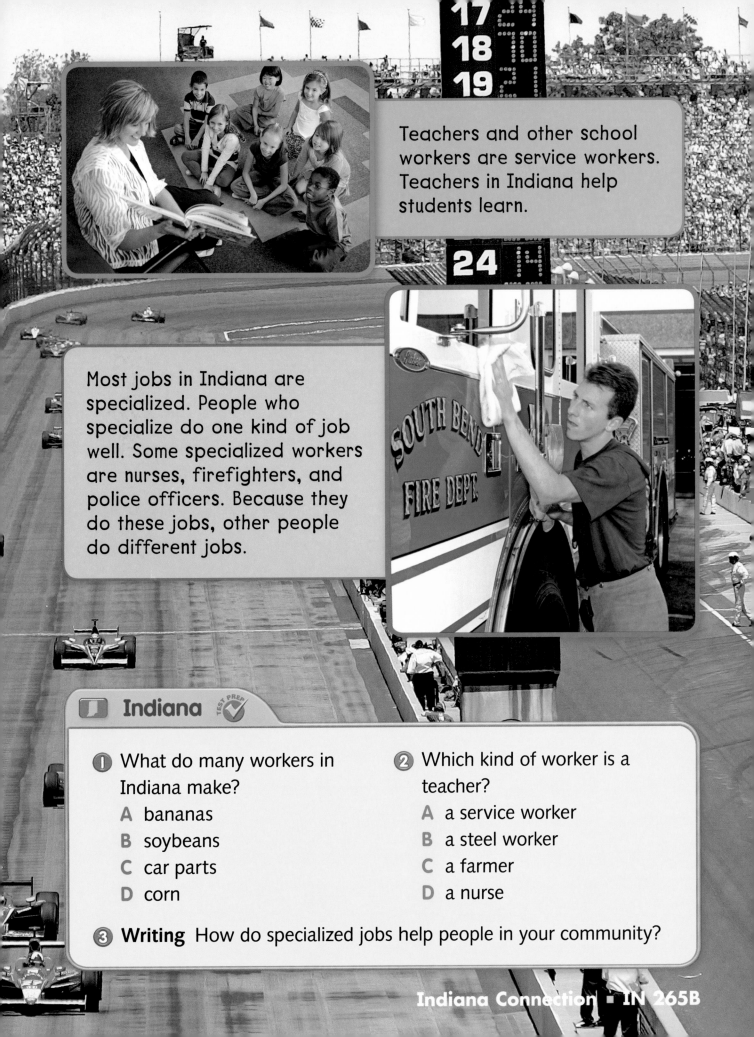

Teachers and other school workers are service workers. Teachers in Indiana help students learn.

Most jobs in Indiana are specialized. People who specialize do one kind of job well. Some specialized workers are nurses, firefighters, and police officers. Because they do these jobs, other people do different jobs.

Indiana TEST PREP

1. What do many workers in Indiana make?
   - A bananas
   - B soybeans
   - C car parts
   - D corn

2. Which kind of worker is a teacher?
   - A a service worker
   - B a steel worker
   - C a farmer
   - D a nurse

3. **Writing** How do specialized jobs help people in your community?

Unit 6 People in the Marketplace

Talk About
Work

" I earned money to buy a gift for my brother. "

"I think about the cost before I choose what I will buy."

"I use money I saved to buy what I want."

265

producer   A person who grows, makes, or sells products. (page 276)

goods   Things that can be bought and sold. (page 277)

services Work done for others. (page 277)

Molly's Pet Store
Order Number 14432
At Molly's, Service Is Number One

Fish Tank	
Goldfish	22.49
Gravel	1.49
Fish Food	2.49
	1.99
4 Items Subtotal	28.46
Sales Tax 6%	1.71
Total	30.17
Cash Payment	31.00
Change	.83

Save all receipts
THANK YOU

marketplace Where people buy and sell goods and services. (page 304)

consumer A person who buys and uses goods and services. (page 279)

GO ONLINE For more resources, go to www.harcourtschool.com/ss1

267

Reading Social Studies
Focus Skill
Categorize and Classify

Why It Matters You can categorize and classify information to help you understand what you read.

Learn

When you categorize and classify, you sort things into groups.

● Decide what each group will be called.

● Place each thing in a group.

Read the paragraph below.

Categorize
Classify

Rob and Mom shopped at the Farmers' Market. They bought fresh food, plants, and toys. The foods they bought were peppers and cucumbers. Mom chose a yellow rosebush and daisies for the garden. Rob bought some toys—a wooden whistle and a puzzle.

When they finished shopping, Mom bought lemonade. Rob bought grape juice.

Practice

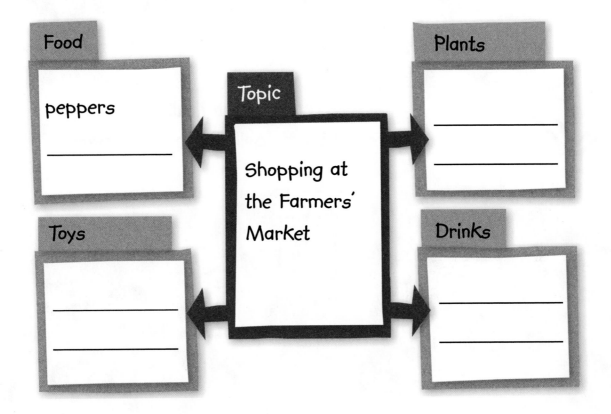

Food
peppers
_____

Plants
_____
_____

Topic

Shopping at the Farmers' Market

Toys
_____
_____

Drinks
_____
_____

Copy this chart to categorize and classify the things that Rob and Mom bought. Put them in four groups labeled Food, Plants, Toys, and Drinks.

Apply

As you read this unit, look for ways to categorize and classify information.

SUPERMARKET

by Kathleen Krull

illustrated by Melanie Hope Greenberg

Shopping carts clang.
Magic doors whiz open and shut.
Colors glow under bright white lights.
So many breakfasts, lunches, and dinners!
It's all at a special, necessary, very real place:
the supermarket.

OATS & MORE

According to surveys, shoppers decide in their first 8 seconds whether they feel comfortable in a store. The first thing they see helps them decide.

The doors don't really open by magic. When an electronic "eye" overhead "sees" you coming, it starts a motor to open the doors.

The supermarket is a whole world of its own. Where does all this crunchy, munchy, sweet, sour, fiery, frozen, fabulous food come from?

Happy Farms

Certain states are famous for certain foods: Iowa for popcorn, Vermont for maple syrup, Michigan for cereal, Wisconsin for cheese, Idaho for potatoes, Massachusetts for cranberries, Florida for oranges, California for grapes, Georgia for peaches and peanuts.

It all begins on farms. Our food comes from places with lots of sunshine, rich soil, and clean water. Farmers make decisions every day during the long months of growing.

At harvesttime, workers pick the fruits and vegetables. They pack everything neatly in boxes and load the boxes onto trucks.

Happy Farms

Ha

Picking fruits and vegetables can be painful, low-paying work. Cesar Chavez (1927-1993) became a hero for workers when he founded the National Farm Workers of America.

273

Small trucks, big trucks, gigantic trucks— all rev up their engines. Every night, drivers take off from farms or warehouses.

274

They zoom down the highway toward your town.

Response Corner

1. **Focus Skill** **Categorize and Classify**   What kinds of things are found in a supermarket?

2. **Make It Relevant**   What are some of the foods your family buys?

What to Know
How do producers and consumers depend on each other?

Vocabulary
producer
goods
services
business
consumer

Categorize and Classify

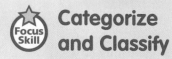

Producers and Consumers

Christina and her family live in a community in which people have many kinds of jobs. Some workers grow or make products, and others sell products. A worker who grows, makes, or sells products is called a **producer**.

Goods and Services

Products are also called goods. **Goods** are things that can be bought and sold. Christina's grandmother grows flowers to sell. Her dad makes parts that are used to make computers.

Producers also provide services. **Services** are work people do for others. Dr. Briggs takes care of Christina's teeth. Mr. West teaches her to play the cello.

(Reading Check) **How are goods and services alike?**

Goods

Services

Buying and Selling

Christina and her mom go shopping downtown. Main Street has many businesses. A person who owns a **business** makes or sells goods or provides services.

Christina gets her hair cut at the salon. She and her mom buy sandals at the shoe store and raisin bread at the bakery. The salon, the shoe store, and the bakery are all businesses.

✂ Hair Salon   ⚘ Shoe Store   🧁 Bakery

Christina and her mom are consumers. A **consumer** is a person who buys goods or services. When consumers buy things, they provide money so producers can buy things. This makes producers consumers, too. The baker buys shoes. The shoe salesperson gets a haircut. The hairstylist buys bread.

 **Reading Check** **Categorize and Classify**

How can a person be both a consumer and a producer?

Summary Producers work to provide consumers with goods and services.

Review

1. **What to Know** How do producers and consumers depend on each other?

2. **Vocabulary** What is a **business** that provides goods in your community?

3. **Activity** Research what goods and services are produced in your community. Then make a chart that shows what you found.

4. **Categorize and Classify** When Christina got her hair cut, did she buy a good or a service?

Read a Bar Graph

Why It Matters Some kinds of information are easier to find in a bar graph. A **bar graph** uses bars to show amounts or numbers of things.

Learn

A bar graph's title tells you the kind of information it shows. Each bar stands for a different group being counted. You read some bar graphs from left to right and others from bottom to top.

Practice

① How many dogs went to the Pet Palace on Tuesday?

② On which day did the Pet Palace groom five dogs?

③ What were the two busiest days at the Pet Palace?

280

Dogs Groomed at the Pet Palace

	0	1	2	3	4	5	6	7
Sunday								
Monday								
Tuesday								
Wednesday								
Thursday								
Friday								
Saturday								

Apply

Make It Relevant Make a bar graph. Show different kinds of pets and the number of people you know who have each kind.

GO ONLINE For online activities, go to **www.harcourtschool.com/ss1**

281

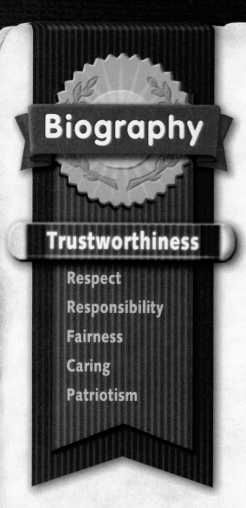

Trustworthiness

Respect
Responsibility
Fairness
Caring
Patriotism

Why Character Counts

Why is it important for a businesswoman like Wanda Montañez to be trustworthy?

Wanda Montañez

Born in Puerto Rico, Wanda Montañez is proud of her native country. When she moved to the United States, she went to many Puerto Rican festivals. She tried to find clothing she could wear to show pride in her Hispanic culture. She knew that others in the Hispanic community felt the same way she did.

Wanda Montañez started her own clothing company.

Wanda Montañez designs clothing that shows Spanish words.

Wanda Montañez decided to create a line of clothing with Spanish words as part of the design. She gets ideas from Latin music and from listening to people talk. Wanda Montañez is helping others learn about her culture through her company's product.

GO ONLINE For more resources, go to www.harcourtschool.com/ss1

Time

1965 | Present
Born

1973 Moves to the United States from Puerto Rico

1986 Graduates from college

2003 Starts her clothing company

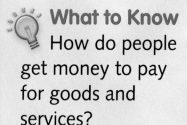
Vocabulary

occupation

income

free enterprise

wants

Categorize and Classify

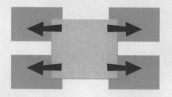

Work and Income

Earning Money

People get paid for making or selling goods or for providing services. An **occupation** is a job a person works at to earn money. The money that people earn is called **income**.

park ranger

People choose occupations in which they can do work they enjoy. Some may be good at singing or teaching. Others may enjoy building things or working with animals. Many people get special training for their jobs.

(Reading Check) **How do people choose their occupations?**

potter

builder

Running a Business

Some people have ideas for businesses of their own. A person who likes to make a product might start a new business to sell that product. The freedom to start and run a business to make money is called **free enterprise**.

Children can take part in free enterprise. They can wash cars, rake leaves, care for pets, and sell things they make. These businesses are all forms of free enterprise. The children who do these jobs earn income.

Reading Check **Focus Skill** **Categorize and Classify** **What are some ways children can take part in free enterprise?**

Children in History

Annie Oakley

Annie Oakley's father died when she was very young. She had to learn to hunt animals for food. To earn money, she sold this food to other people in Cincinnati, Ohio. The income helped her family buy the things they needed. Later, Annie Oakley won many medals for her shooting skills.

Spending Money

People use their income to buy goods and services. They may also save some of it. They use their money to pay for wants. **Wants** are things that people would like to have. Pets, books, and new bicycles are wants. Some wants are needs. A home, food, and clothing are needs.

People cannot buy everything they want. They have to make choices about what things are important to them. Most people first buy the goods and services that will keep them safe and comfortable. Then they buy other goods and services they would like to have.

Reading Check **How do people decide what goods and services to buy?**

Summary People work so that they can earn income to buy goods and services.

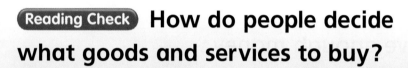

1. **What to Know** How do people get money to pay for goods and services?

2. **Vocabulary** What do people do with **income**?

3. ✏️ **Write** Make a list of things you like to do. Choose one that you could do to earn income.

4. (Focus Skill) **Categorize and Classify** Write down the occupations of family members or adult friends. Circle the ones in which people make goods.

Make a Choice When Buying

Why It Matters Many times, goods you want cost more money than you have.

Learn

When you do not have enough money to buy everything you want, you have to make a choice. What you choose not to buy is called the opportunity cost.

A budget can help you choose what you buy. A **budget** is a plan that shows how much money you have and how much money you spend.

Using a budget, you can also save money. Money not spent on goods and services is called savings. You can put your savings in a bank. A **bank** is a business that keeps money safe.

290

Practice

Imagine that you have earned ten dollars. You want to see a movie. You also want to buy new skates. You will have to make a choice about spending or saving your money.

1 If you see the movie, what will you give up?

2 If you decide to save for skates, what will you give up?

Apply

Make It Relevant If you had ten dollars, would you spend the money right away or save it? Why?

Points of View

The Sidewalk Reporter asks:

"How do you make sure that you spend your money wisely?"

Carlos

"I put $25 in a jar to spend each week on extras."

Rick

"I'm saving for a dirt bike, so I don't spend a penny of what I earn."

View from the Past

The First Bank

After the American Revolution, each state still used its own kind of money. Leaders started a bank in Philadelphia that would create one form of money for the United States.

Mrs. Walker

"I make a list of the things I want to buy to be sure they fit in my budget."

Ms. Benitez

"When I want to buy something, I wait a week to make sure I really want it."

Mr. Johnson

"I use my money to pay my bills, and I save the rest."

It's Your Turn

- Do you do any of the things these citizens do? If so, which ones?
- How do you make sure that you spend your money wisely?

293

From Factory to You

What to Know
How do raw materials become products?

Vocabulary

raw material

factory

human resources

capital resources

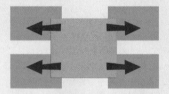

Categorize and Classify
Focus Skill

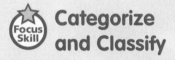

Daniel wanted a new baseball bat for his birthday. His grandfather took him to the Louisville Slugger Museum and Bat Factory in Louisville, Kentucky. Together they learned how wooden bats are made.

Louisville Slugger Museum in Louisville, Kentucky

A Bat's Beginning

The making of a bat begins in a forest of trees. Trees are **raw materials**, or natural resources used to make a product.

First, the trees are cut into many long sections. Next, the wood is dried. Then, the wood is shipped to the places where the bats are made.

Reading Check **What raw material is used to make a baseball bat?**

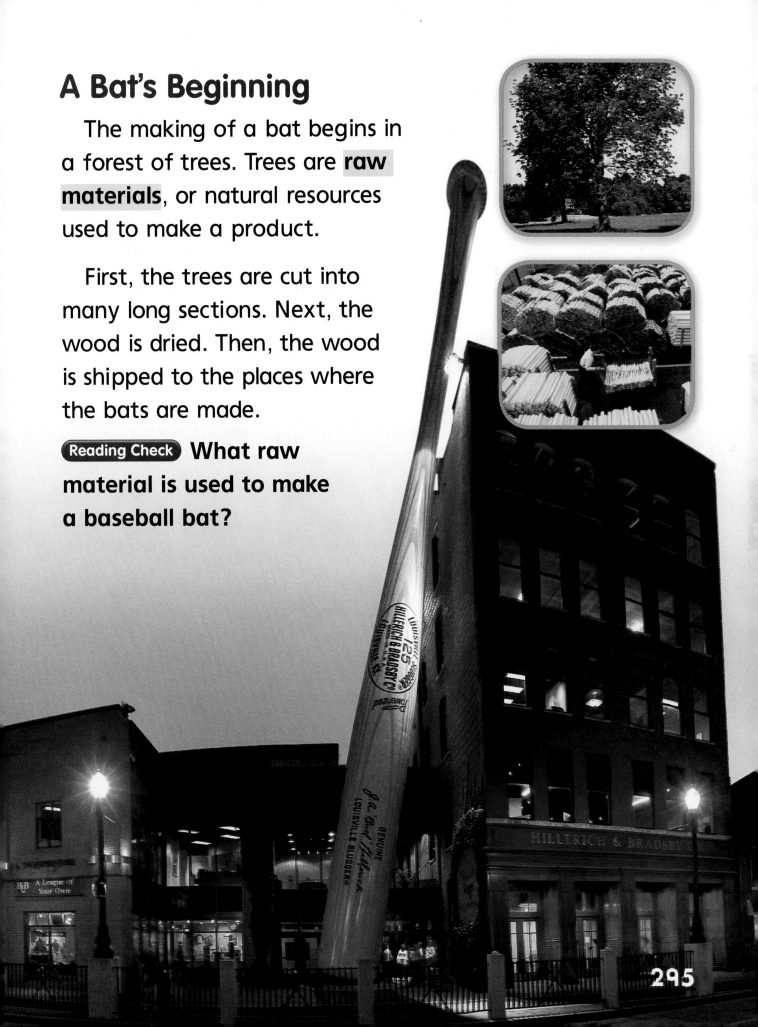

At the Factory

Baseball bats are goods that are made in factories. A **factory** is a building in which people use machines to make goods.

Many people work at the factory doing different jobs to make the bats. The work these people do is called **human resources**.

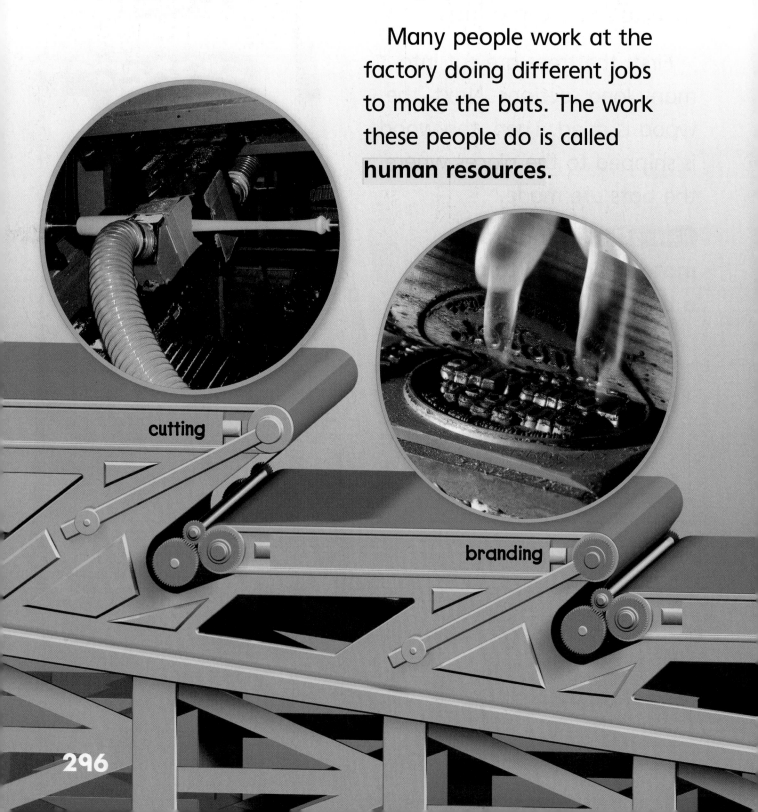

cutting

branding

All of the tools used to produce a good are called **capital resources**. At the factory, the wood is first placed in a machine that cuts it into a bat shape. After the bats are cut, they are branded. A worker burns the name of the company onto the bat. Then the bats are sanded and stained a certain color. Last, the bats are packaged. They are ready to be sold.

Reading Check **How is the wood changed when it is made into a bat at the factory?**

sanding

Louisville Slugger Bats

packaging

To the Market

The bats are finally ready for markets where people will buy them. The bats are moved to markets in many ways. Trucks or trains may deliver the bats to places around the United States. Airplanes may be used to take the bats to places around the world.

Louisville Slugger® Bats

At a sporting goods store, Daniel and his grandfather find the bat they want to buy. The money they pay for the bat will be used to make more bats.

Reading Check **Categorize and Classify**
How are goods, such as bats, taken to markets?

Summary Human and capital resources are used to change raw materials into products to be sold.

Review

1 **What to Know** How do raw materials become products?

2 **Vocabulary** How does a company use its **capital resources**?

3 **Activity** Choose a raw material that comes from your community or state. Make a poster to show the things that can be made from it.

4 **Categorize and Classify** What is the difference between a capital resource and a human resource?

299

Read a Flowchart

Why It Matters   A **flowchart** shows the steps needed to make or do something. You can use a flowchart to show the steps workers follow to make a product.

Learn

The title of the flowchart tells what it is about. Each picture has a sentence that tells about the step. The arrows show the order of the steps.

Practice

❶ What does the flowchart on the next page show?

❷ What is the first step?

❸ What happens after the bats are made at the factory?

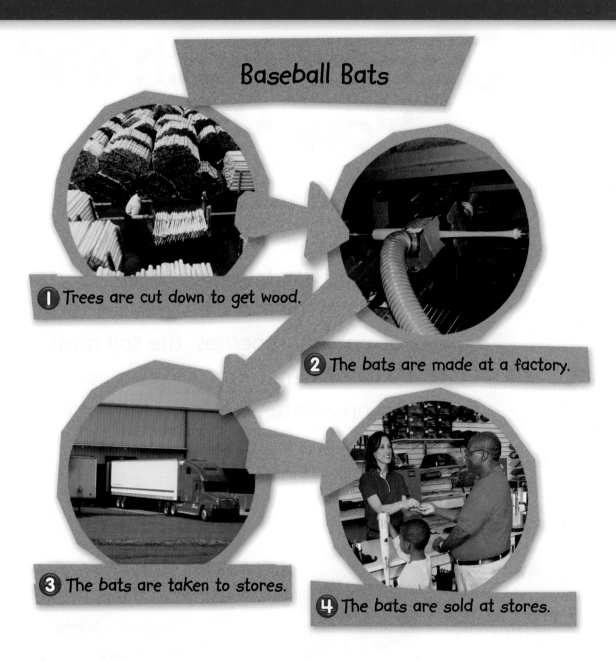

Baseball Bats

1. Trees are cut down to get wood.

2. The bats are made at a factory.

3. The bats are taken to stores.

4. The bats are sold at stores.

Apply

Make It Relevant Make a flowchart showing the steps for something you do everyday.

GO ONLINE

For online activities, go to
www.harcourtschool.com/ss1

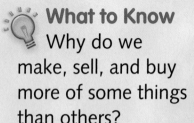
What to Know
Why do we make, sell, and buy more of some things than others?

Vocabulary

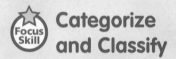
scarce

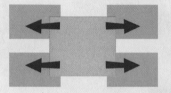
marketplace

Focus Skill **Categorize and Classify**

How Much and How Many?

Producing Goods

Grace lives in New Jersey. Her family grows blueberries for products such as blueberry muffins. For good blueberries, the soil must be rich. There must also be enough sun and water, and the blueberry bushes must be healthy.

Blueberry bushes in New Jersey

Farmers who grow blueberries can face problems. Without enough water, the berries can dry out in the hot summer sun. Too much rain can harm the blueberries, too. Cold weather can freeze the berries.

drought

If any of these things happen, blueberries will be scarce. When something is **scarce**, there is not enough of it to meet everyone's wants.

Reading Check **What problems do farmers who grow blueberries face?**

flood

High and Low Prices

In the marketplace, the price of goods can go up and down. The **marketplace** is where goods and services are bought and sold. A price is what people pay when they buy a good or service. If there are not many blueberries and many people want to buy them, the price will go up. If there are many blueberries, or if not many people want them, the price will go down.

Whole Blueberry Pie $8

Blueberry Muffins $1 each

Sometimes goods are scarce because there are few raw materials to make them. Other times, the raw materials cost too much. Goods can also be scarce if they take a long time to make. People have to pay more money to buy things that are scarce.

Reading Check **Why might the price of something go up?**

Summary When there is a lot of a product, people will pay less. When a product is scarce, they will pay more.

Fast Fact!

A new <u>The Cat in the Hat</u> book costs $8.99. Copies of the first printing of this book are scarce. The price of this old book can be thousands of dollars.

THE CAT IN THE HAT

By Dr. Seuss

Review

1. **What to Know** Why do we make, sell, and buy more of some things than others?

2. **Vocabulary** What will happen to the cost of blueberry muffins if blueberries are **scarce**?

3. **Write** Imagine that you are a farmer. Write about something that has caused your crop to fail.

4. **(Focus Skill) Categorize and Classify** Look around your classroom. Make a list of things that are made from the same raw material.

305

Preview and Question

Why It Matters   New ideas are easier to understand when you read to answer questions.

Learn

A K-W-L chart helps you record important facts before and after you read. The K-W-L chart on the next page shows what Marco knows about scarce goods. Copy the chart.

Practice

Read the paragraph. Then add new facts to the K-W-L chart.

Sometimes a country's supply of a product is not enough to meet the demand for it. This is called scarcity. When a product is scarce, the country can import it. To import a product means to get it from another country. Countries can also import the resources needed to make the product.

K-W-L Chart

What I Know	What I Want to Know	What I Learned
Sometimes the supply of a product is not enough to meet the demand for it.	How can we get goods that are scarce?	
Sometimes there are not enough resources to make a product.	How can we get resources that are scarce?	

Apply

Make It Relevant Make a K-W-L chart to show what you know and want to know about scarcity and importing. As you read the next lesson, add facts to show what you have learned.

Barter and Trade

What to Know
How does trade help people meet their needs?

Vocabulary
barter
trade

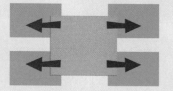

Categorize and Classify

In the past, people would exchange their goods or services with others to get things they needed. They would barter with each other. To **barter** is to exchange things without using money.

Bartering long ago

308

Using Money

It can be hard to find people to barter with for the goods and services you need when you need them. Over time, people began to use money to buy and sell their goods and services. The buyer and seller agree on a fair price for a good or service.

Barter and money are both used to make a trade. A **trade** is the exchange of one thing for another.

Reading Check What can people use to make trades with each other?

Money now has different forms.

People using money today

Trading with Other Countries

The people of a country cannot always provide all the goods and services that citizens want. These people can trade with people in other countries to get raw materials, goods, or services. To get those, they may give other raw materials, goods, services, or money.

Reading Check **Why do the people of a country trade with people of another country?**

Products come into and go out of this port in New Jersey.

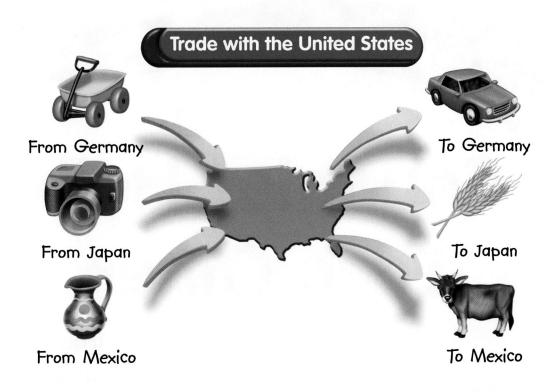

Trade with the United States

From Germany

From Japan

From Mexico

To Germany

To Japan

To Mexico

What is a product that the United States gets from another country?

Summary People can trade raw materials, goods, services, or money with one another.

Review

1 **What to Know** How does trade help people meet their needs?

2 **Vocabulary** What do you do when you **barter**?

3 **Activity** Draw pictures and write labels that show goods you would be willing to trade.

4 **Categorize and Classify** Make a list of goods and services you and your classmates could use to barter. Circle the services.

Countries Help Each Other

You have learned that countries trade with each other to get goods and services. Now read about how countries help each other in times of need.

When an earthquake caused powerful ocean waves to hit countries in Asia, many people lost their homes, schools, and businesses. Students at Pleasant Ridge Elementary School in Saline, Michigan, wanted to help. They decided to collect spare change. They raised more than two thousand dollars!

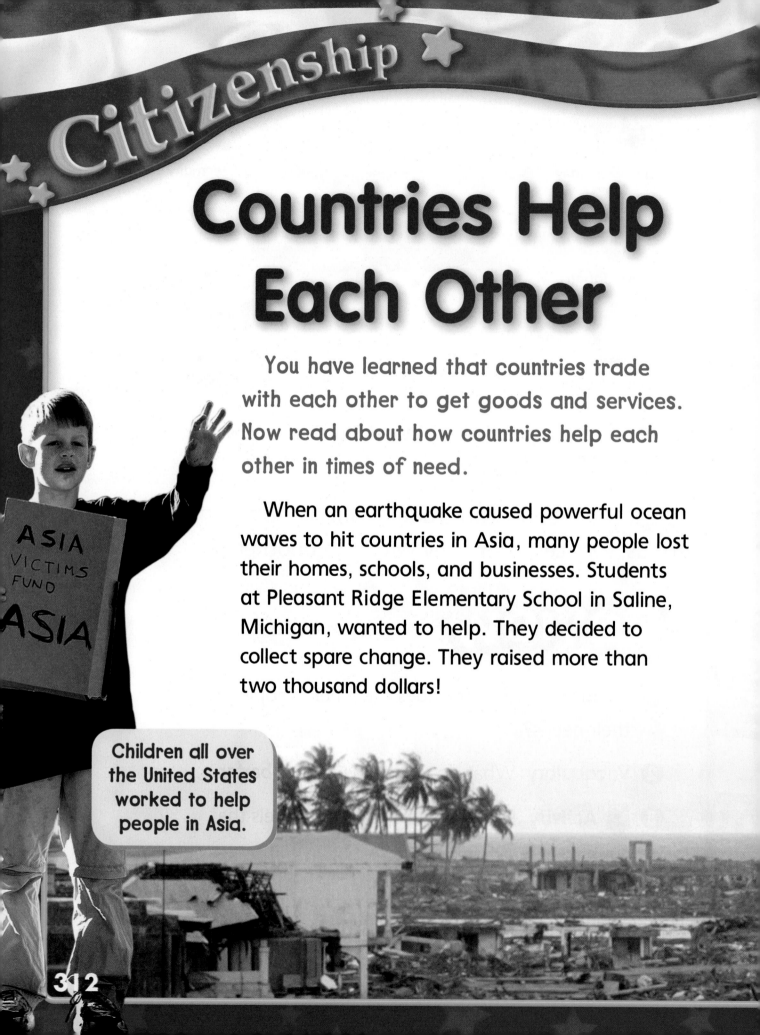

ASIA VICTIMS FUND ASIA

Children all over the United States worked to help people in Asia.

The students at Pleasant Ridge gave the money they raised to the American Red Cross. The Red Cross is a group that sends supplies and volunteers to help in disasters.

The United States government also helped the people in Asia by sending money. Many countries send money, supplies, and volunteers to help people in need around the world.

Make It Relevant What could you do to help people in disasters?

The American Red Cross helps people in our country and other countries.

Marketplace

ICE CREAM

CONES

T-SHIRT SALE

FRESH PRODUCE

SANDWICH

LEMONADE

Face
Painting

PIZZA

314

Look at the picture.

What goods do these people sell?

Who is offering a service?

Online GO Adventures

Play an online shopping game with Eco. You will help him spend money wisely at a shop, a restaurant, and an arcade. Play now, at www.harcourtschool.com/ss1

PLANTS

315

Review and Test Prep

 The Big Idea

Work Producers and consumers depend on each other for goods and services.

Focus Skill Categorize and Classify

Copy and fill in the chart to categorize and classify what you learned about the goods and services producers provide.

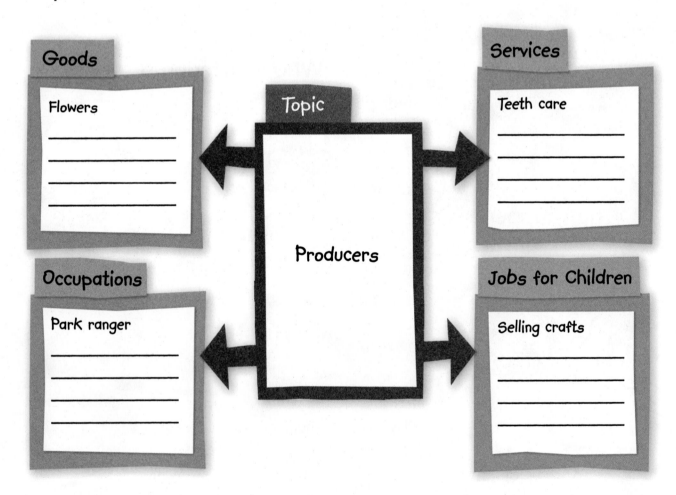

Goods

Flowers
_____
_____
_____

Topic

Producers

Services

Teeth care
_____
_____
_____

Occupations

Park ranger
_____
_____
_____

Jobs for Children

Selling crafts
_____
_____
_____
_____

Vocabulary

Match the word to its meaning.

1. things that can be bought and sold

2. work done for others

3. a place where goods are sold

4. a person who buys goods and services

5. a worker who grows, makes, or sells goods

Word Bank

producer
(p. 276)

goods
(p. 277)

services
(p. 277)

consumer
(p. 279)

marketplace
(p. 304)

Facts and Main Ideas

6. What do we call the job a person does to earn money?

7. Why do people earn income?

8. What happens in a factory?

9. What do you call all the tools used to produce a good?

   A human resources   **C** services

   B raw materials   **D** capital resources

10. Which means to exchange something without using money?

    A barter   **C** consumer

    B occupation   **D** free enterprise

⑪ What would happen if the United States could not trade with other countries?

⑫ **Make It Relevant** How would your life be different if your family had to produce all of the goods it wanted?

Skills

June Bicycle Sales

Week 1	
Week 2	
Week 3	
Week 4	

0 1 2 3 4 5 6 7

⑬ What is the title of this bar graph?

⑭ How many bicycles were sold in Week 2?

⑮ Which week had the most sales?

⑯ Which week had the fewest sales?

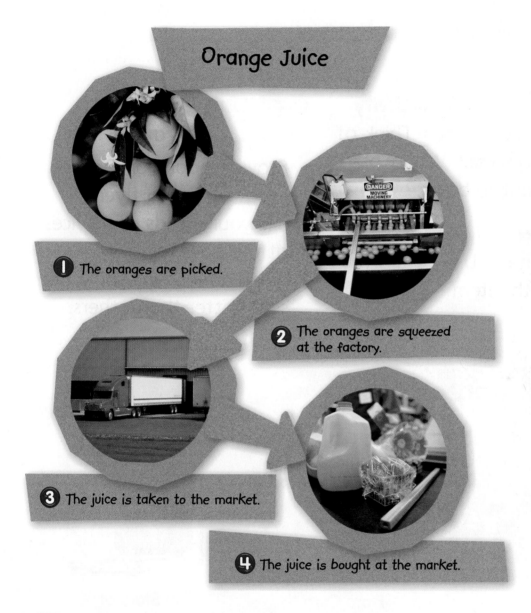

Orange Juice

① The oranges are picked.

② The oranges are squeezed at the factory.

③ The juice is taken to the market.

④ The juice is bought at the market.

⑰ What does this flowchart show?

⑱ What is the first step?

⑲ What happens after the oranges are squeezed?

⑳ What happens after the juice is taken to the market?

319

Activities

Show What You Know

Unit Writing Activity

Create a Sales Pitch Think of something to sell. Why would others want to buy it?

Write an Ad Write an ad to sell your item. Use details to describe the item.

Unit Project

Class Fair Plan a class fair.

- Provide goods or services.
- Create ads and flyers.
- Sell your goods or services at the class fair.
- Think about why some items sold better than others.

Read More

Delivery
by Anastasia Suen

Puffin Books

From Corn to Cereal
by Roberta Basel

Capstone Press

The Story of Money
by Betsy Maestro

Clarion Books/Houghton Mifflin Company

For more resources, go to
www.harcourtschool.com/ss1

320

For Your Reference

ATLAS

RESEARCH HANDBOOK

BIOGRAPHICAL DICTIONARY

PICTURE GLOSSARY

INDEX

For Your Reference

Atlas

Research Handbook

Biographical Dictionary

Picture Glossary

Index

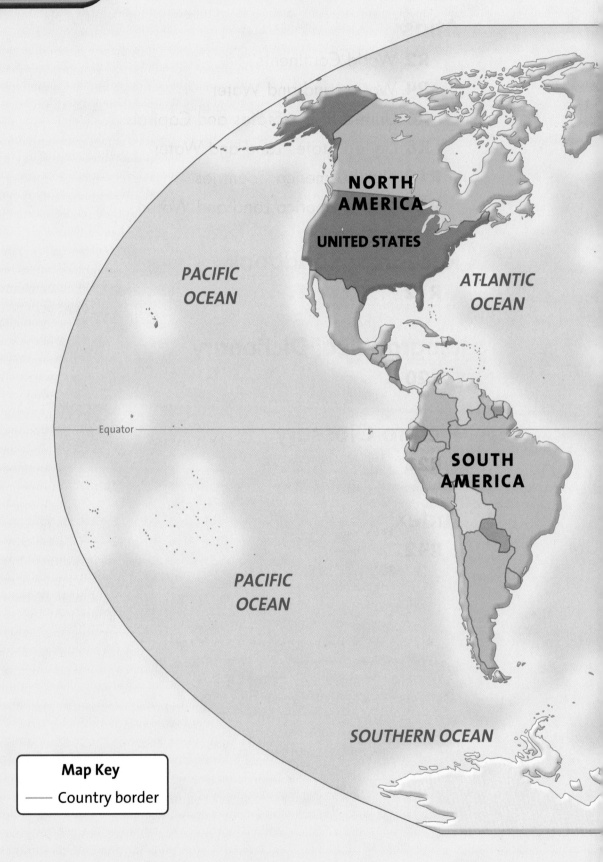

NORTH
AMERICA

UNITED STATES

PACIFIC
OCEAN

ATLANTIC
OCEAN

Equator

SOUTH
AMERICA

PACIFIC
OCEAN

SOUTHERN OCEAN

Map Key

—— Country border

ARCTIC OCEAN

EUROPE

ASIA

PACIFIC
OCEAN

AFRICA

ATLANTIC
OCEAN

INDIAN
OCEAN

North

West ✦ East

South

AUSTRALIA

0   1,000   2,000 Miles
0   1,000   2,000 Kilometers

SOUTHERN OCEAN

ANTARCTICA

R3

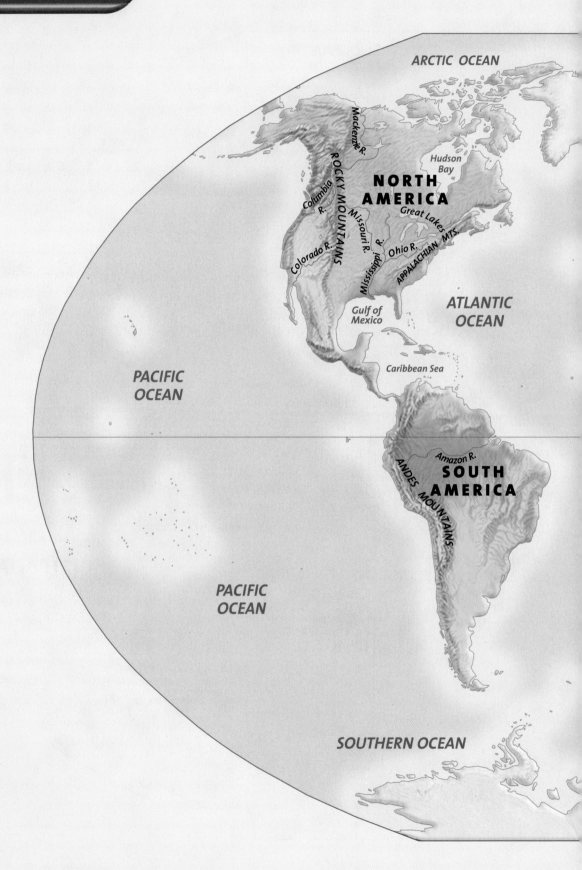

ARCTIC OCEAN

Mackenzie R.

ROCKY MOUNTAINS

Columbia R.

Colorado R.

Missouri R.

Mississippi R.

Ohio R.

Hudson Bay

NORTH AMERICA

Great Lakes

APPALACHIAN MTS.

Gulf of Mexico

PACIFIC OCEAN

Caribbean Sea

ATLANTIC OCEAN

Amazon R.

ANDES MOUNTAINS

SOUTH AMERICA

PACIFIC OCEAN

SOUTHERN OCEAN

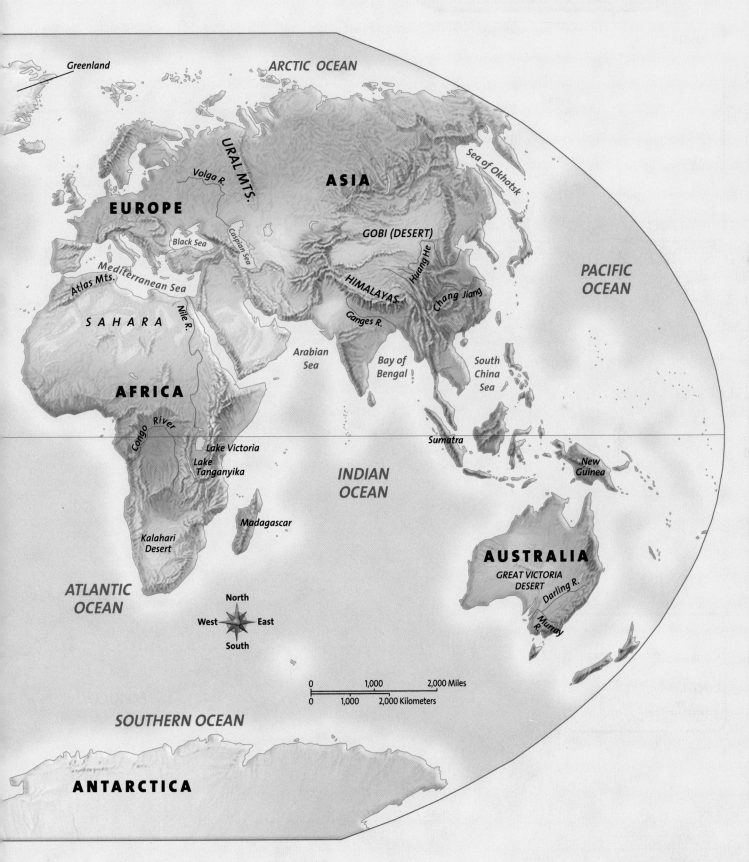

Greenland

ARCTIC OCEAN

URAL MTS.

Volga R.

EUROPE

ASIA

Sea of Okhotsk

Black Sea

Caspian Sea

GOBI (DESERT)

Huang He

Mediterranean Sea

Atlas Mts.

HIMALAYAS

Chang Jiang

PACIFIC
OCEAN

SAHARA

Nile R.

Ganges R.

AFRICA

Arabian
Sea

Bay of
Bengal

South
China
Sea

Congo River

Lake Victoria

Sumatra

Lake
Tanganyika

INDIAN
OCEAN

New
Guinea

Madagascar

ATLANTIC
OCEAN

Kalahari
Desert

AUSTRALIA

GREAT VICTORIA
DESERT

Darling R.

North

Murray R.

West   East

South

0   1,000   2,000 Miles

0   1,000   2,000 Kilometers

SOUTHERN OCEAN

ANTARCTICA

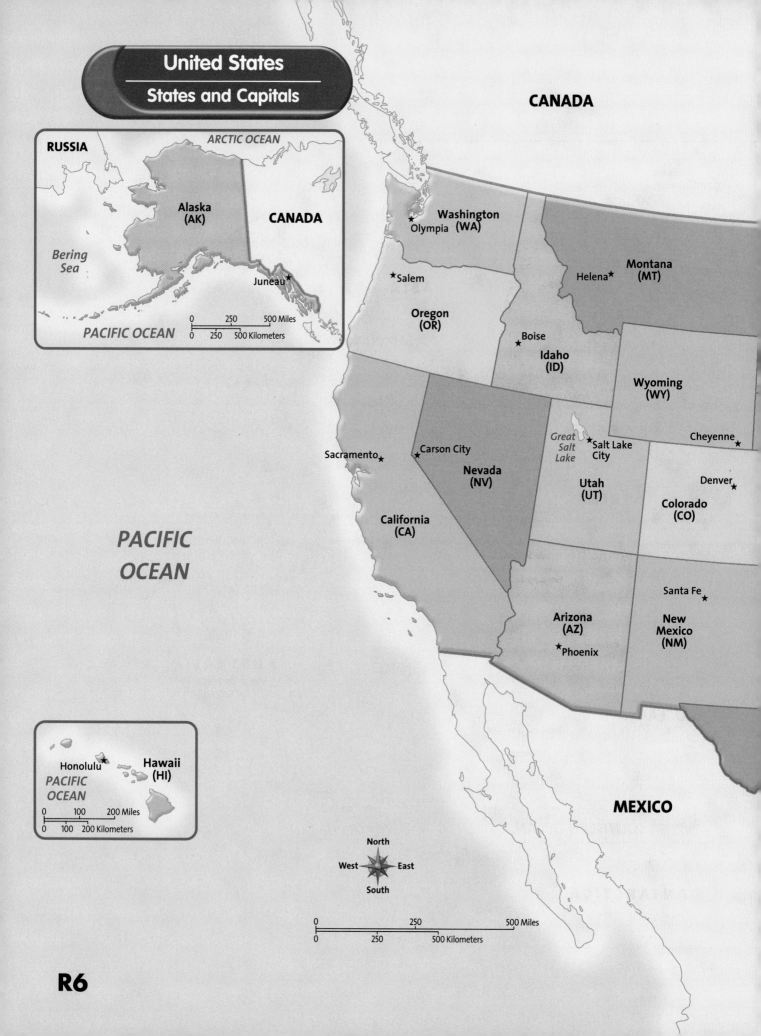

United States
States and Capitals

RUSSIA

ARCTIC OCEAN

Alaska (AK)

CANADA

Bering Sea

★ Juneau

PACIFIC OCEAN

0   250   500 Miles
0   250   500 Kilometers

PACIFIC OCEAN

Honolulu ★
Hawaii (HI)
PACIFIC OCEAN

0   100   200 Miles
0   100   200 Kilometers

CANADA

★ Olympia   Washington (WA)

★ Salem

Oregon (OR)

Helena ★   Montana (MT)

★ Boise   Idaho (ID)

Wyoming (WY)

Cheyenne ★

Great Salt Lake   ★ Salt Lake City

Sacramento ★   ★ Carson City   Nevada (NV)   Utah (UT)   Denver ★

Colorado (CO)

California (CA)

Santa Fe ★

Arizona (AZ)   New Mexico (NM)

★ Phoenix

MEXICO

North
West — East
South

0   250   500 Miles
0   250   500 Kilometers

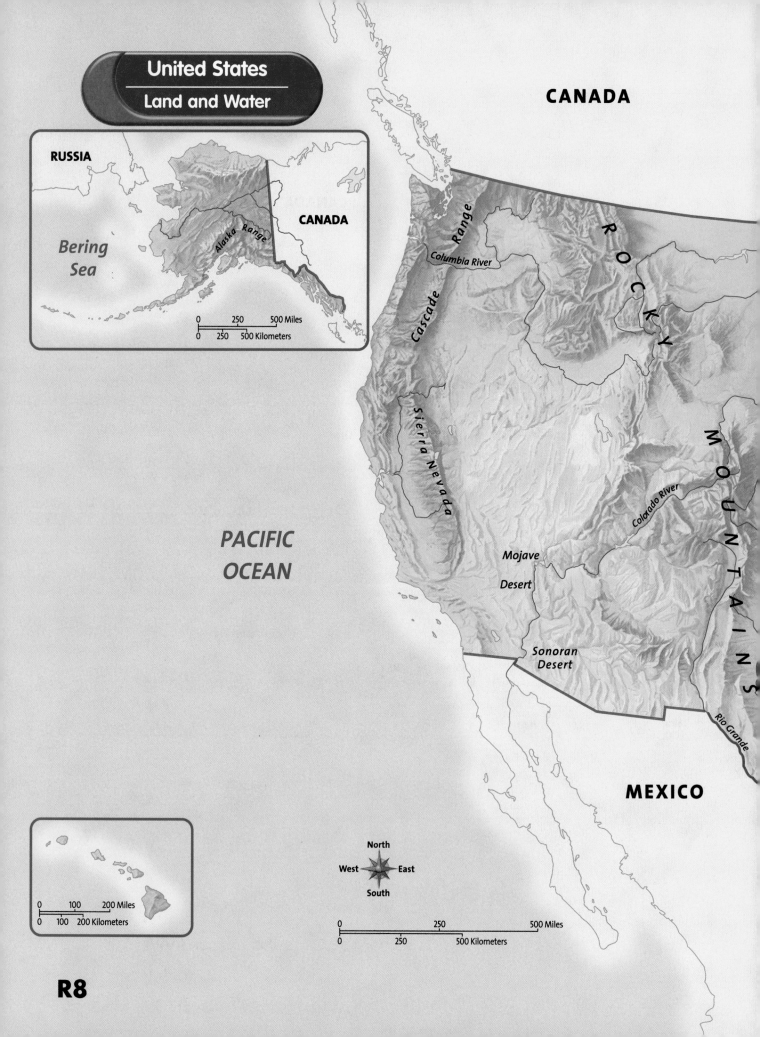

United States
Land and Water

RUSSIA

CANADA

Bering
Sea

Alaska Range

0   250   500 Miles
0   250   500 Kilometers

CANADA

R O C K Y

Columbia River

Cascade Range

Sierra Nevada

Colorado River

Mojave
Desert

Sonoran
Desert

M O U N T A I N S

Rio Grande

PACIFIC

OCEAN

MEXICO

0   100   200 Miles
0   100   200 Kilometers

North

West   East

South

0   250   500 Miles
0   250   500 Kilometers

CANADA

Lake Superior

Lake Huron

Lake Michigan

Lake Ontario

Lake Erie

G R E A T   P L A I N S

Missouri River

Mississippi River

INTERIOR
PLAINS

Missouri River

Ohio River

A P P A L A C H I A N   M O U N T A I N S

Mississippi River

ATLANTIC
OCEAN

C O A S T A L   P L A I N

Rio Grande

Gulf of
Mexico

Straits of Florida

BAHAMAS

CUBA

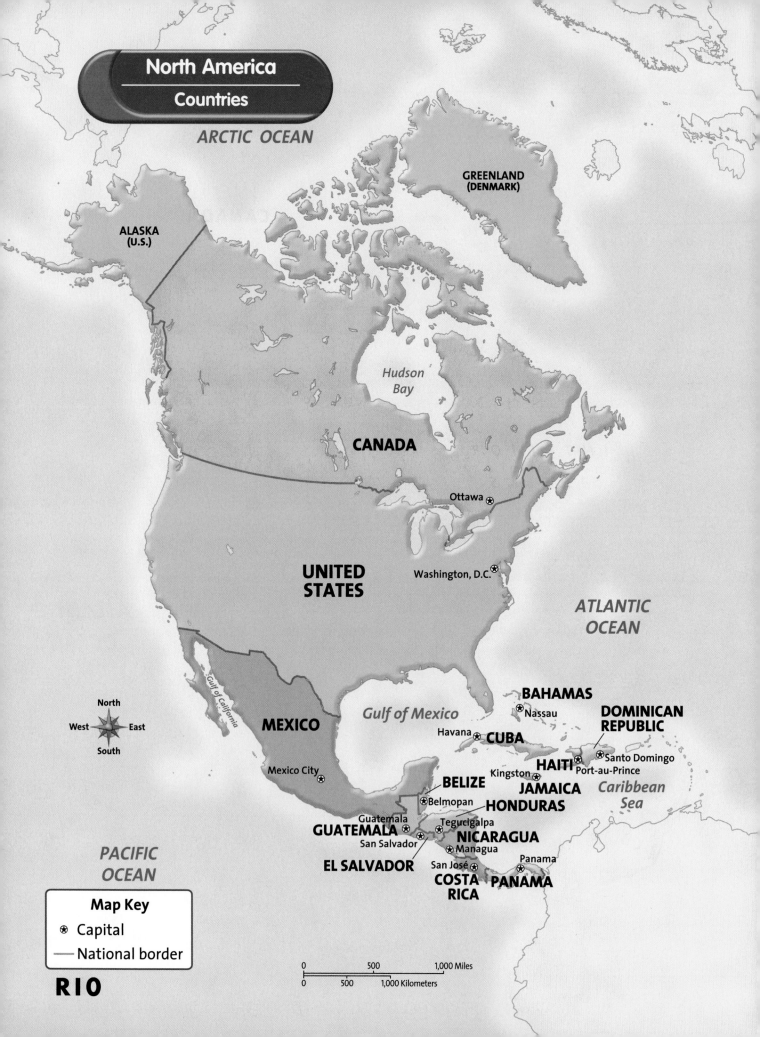

North America
Countries

ARCTIC OCEAN

GREENLAND
(DENMARK)

ALASKA
(U.S.)

*Hudson
Bay*

CANADA

Ottawa ⊛

Washington, D.C. ⊛

UNITED
STATES

ATLANTIC
OCEAN

Gulf of California

North
West — East
South

MEXICO

Gulf of Mexico

BAHAMAS
⊛ Nassau

DOMINICAN
REPUBLIC

Havana ⊛ CUBA

Santo Domingo
⊛
HAITI
Port-au-Prince

Mexico City ⊛

Kingston

JAMAICA

*Caribbean
Sea*

BELIZE
⊛ Belmopan

HONDURAS

Guatemala
⊛
GUATEMALA ⊛
San Salvador

Tegucigalpa
⊛

NICARAGUA
⊛ Managua

EL SALVADOR

San José ⊛

Panama
⊛

PACIFIC
OCEAN

COSTA
RICA

PANAMA

Map Key
⊛ Capital
— National border

0   500   1,000 Miles
0 500 1,000 Kilometers

R10

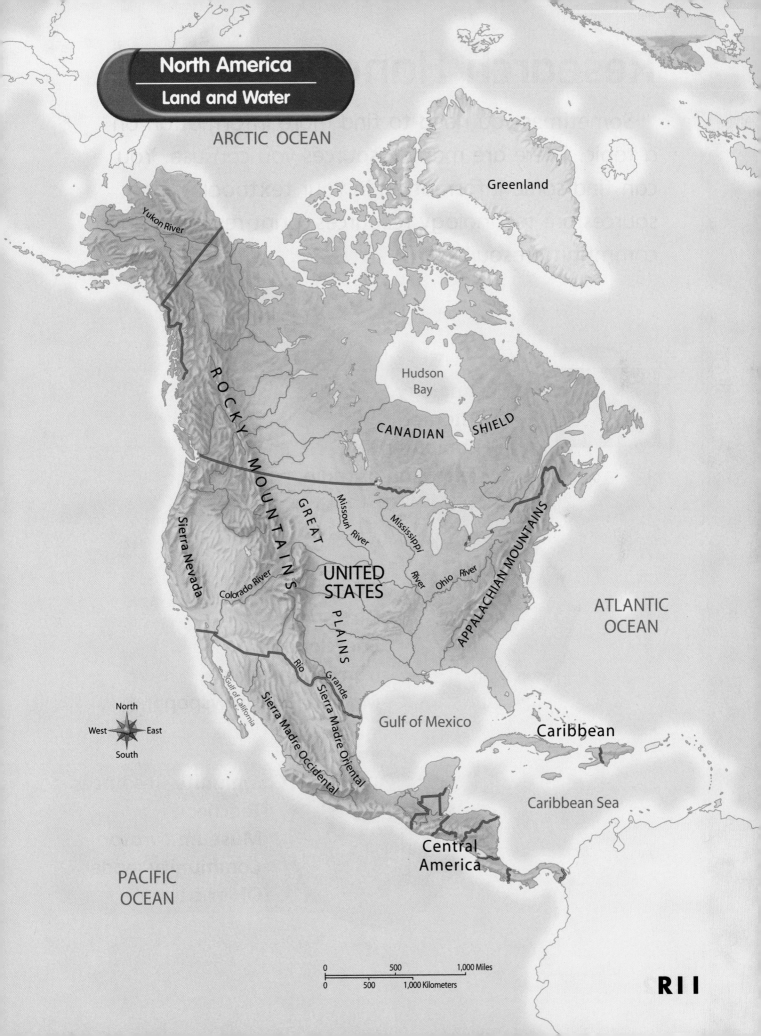

North America
Land and Water

ARCTIC OCEAN

Greenland

Yukon River

Hudson Bay

CANADIAN SHIELD

ROCKY MOUNTAINS

GREAT PLAINS

Sierra Nevada

Colorado River

Missouri River

Mississippi River

Ohio River

UNITED STATES

APPALACHIAN MOUNTAINS

ATLANTIC OCEAN

Rio Grande

Sierra Madre Occidental

Sierra Madre Oriental

Gulf of California

Gulf of Mexico

Caribbean

Caribbean Sea

North
West — East
South

Central America

PACIFIC OCEAN

| 0 | 500 | 1,000 Miles |
| 0 | 500 | 1,000 Kilometers |

R11

Research Handbook

Sometimes you need to find more information on a topic. There are many resources you can use. You can find some information in your textbook. Other sources are technology resources, print resources, and community resources.

Technology Resources
- **Internet**
- **Computer disk**
- **Television or radio**

Print Resources
- **Atlas**
- **Dictionary**
- **Encyclopedia**
- **Nonfiction book**
- **Magazine or newspaper**

Community Resources
- **Teacher**
- **Museum curator**
- **Community leader**
- **Older citizen**

Technology Resources

The main technology resources you can use are the Internet and computer disks. Television and radio can also be good sources of information.

Using the Internet

Information on the Internet is always changing. Be sure to use a site you can trust.

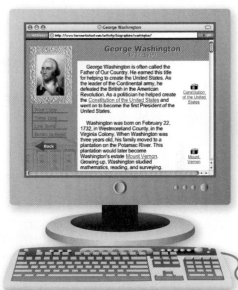

Finding Information

- Use a mouse and a keyboard to search for information.
- With help from a teacher, parent, or older child, find the source you want to search.
- Type in key words.
- Read carefully and take notes.
- If your computer is connected to a printer, you can print out a paper copy.

Print Resources

Books in libraries are placed in a special order. Each book has a call number. The call number tells you where to look for the book.

Some print resources, such as encyclopedias, magazines, and newspapers are kept together in a separate place. Librarians can help you find what you need.

Atlas

An atlas is a book of maps. Some atlases show the same place at different times.

Dictionary

A dictionary gives the correct spelling of words. It also tells you their definitions or what they mean. Words in a dictionary are listed in alphabetical order. Guide words at the tops of the pages help you find the word you are looking for.

Guide Words

dictionary (dictionaries)
A dictionary is a book where you can find out what a word means and how to spell it.

die (dying, died)
When someone or something dies, they stop living.
Plants die without water.

different
If something is different from something else, it is not like it in some way.
Our pens are different. Mine is red and yours is blue.

difficult
Difficult things are not easy to do.
This is a difficult tree to climb.

dig (digging, dug)
To dig means to move soil away to make a hole in the ground.
The dog dug a hole to bury his bone.

dinner (dinners)
Dinner is the main meal of the day.

dinosaur (dinosaurs)
A dinosaur is a large reptile that lived millions of years ago.
(See more **Dinosaurs** on page 123.)

direction (directions)
1 A direction is the way you go to get somewhere.
The school is in that direction.
2 Directions are words or pictures that tell you what to do.
Read the directions on the bottle.

dirt
Dirt is dust or mud.
Wash that dirt off your knees.

dirty (dirtier, dirtiest)
Something that is dirty is covered with mud, food or other marks.
My clothes always get dirty when I play soccer.

disappear (disappearing, disappeared)
If something disappears, you cannot see it any longer.
My toy has disappeared.

disappointed
If someone is disappointed, they feel sad because something they were hoping for did not happen.
Jessica was disappointed when her best friend could not come to her party.

disaster (disasters)
A disaster is something very bad that happens suddenly.
The storm was a disaster. Thousands of trees were blown down.

30

discover (discovering, discovered)
When you discover something, you find out about it.
I've discovered a secret drawer.

discuss (discussing, discussed)
When people discuss things, they talk about them.
We discussed the best way to build the tree house.

dish (dishes)
1 A dish is for cooking or serving food.
2 The dishes are all the things that have to be washed up after a meal.

dishwasher (dishwashers)
A dishwasher is a machine that washes the dishes.

distance (distances)
The distance between two places is how far they are from each other.
The distance between my house and the bus stop is half a mile.

disturb (disturbing, disturbed)
If you disturb someone, you interrupt what they are doing.
Grandma does not like to be disturbed when she is resting.

dive (diving, dived)
If you dive, you jump head first into water.
I can swim, but I can't dive yet.

divide (dividing, divided)
1 If you divide something, you make it into smaller pieces.
Divide the cake into six pieces.
2 When you divide numbers, you find out how many times one goes into another.
Six divided by two is three.

doctor (doctors)
A doctor is someone whose job is to help sick people get better.

dog (dogs)
A dog is an animal that people keep as a pet or to do work. There are many different kinds of dogs.

31

Encyclopedia

An encyclopedia is a book or set of books that gives information about many different topics. The topics are listed in alphabetical order. You can also find encyclopedias on the Internet.

Nonfiction Books

A nonfiction book gives facts about real people, places, and things. Nonfiction books in the library are grouped by subject. Each subject has a different call number. Look in a card file or computer catalog to find a call number. You can look for titles, authors, or subjects.

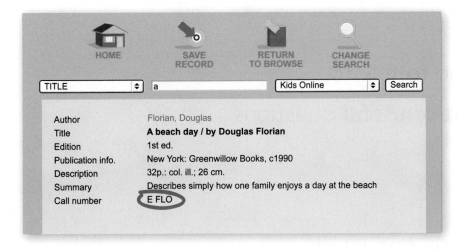

Magazines and Newspapers

Magazines and newspapers are printed by the day, week, or month. They are good sources of the latest information. Many libraries have a guide that lists articles by subject. Two guides are the Children's Magazine Guide and the Readers' Guide to Periodical Literature.

Community Resources

Often, people in your community can give you information you need. Before you talk to anyone, always ask a teacher or a parent for permission.

Listening to Find Information

Before

- Decide who to talk to.
- Make a list of useful questions.

During

- Be polite.
- Speak clearly and loudly.
- Listen carefully. You may think of other questions you want to ask.

- Take notes to help you remember ideas.
- Write down or tape record the person's exact words for quotes. Get permission to use the quotes.
- Later, write a thank-you letter.

Writing to Get Information

You can also write to people in your community to gather information. Keep these ideas in mind as you write:

- Write neatly or use a computer.
- Say who you are and why you are writing.
- Carefully check your spelling and punctuation.
- If you are mailing the letter, put in an addressed, stamped envelope for the person to send you an answer.
- Thank the person.

Biographical Dictionary

The Biographical Dictionary lists many of the important people in this book. They are listed in alphabetical (ABC) order by last name. After each name are the birth and death dates. If the person is still alive, only the birth year is given. The page number tells where the main discussion of each person starts. See the Index for other page references.

Anthony, Susan B. (1820–1906) Women's rights leader. She helped get women the same rights that men have. p. 30

Anyokah Daughter of Sequoyah. When she was six years old, she helped her father create a writing system for the Cherokee people. p. 16

Armstrong, Neil (1930–) American astronaut. He was the first person to walk on the moon. p. 201

Banneker, Benjamin (1731–1806) African American scientist and writer. He helped plan the streets of Washington, D.C. p. 72

Bunyan, Paul A lumberjack of huge size and strength in American legends. His footprints are said to have created Minnesota's 10,000 lakes. p. 201

Bush, George W. (1946–) The 43rd President of the United States. p. 35

Carson, Rachel (1907–1964) American writer. Her books told people how to take better care of nature. p. 122

Carver, George W. (1864–1943) African American scientist. He worked on ways to make farming better in the South. p. 255

Chapman, John (1774–1835) American pioneer known as Johnny Appleseed. He planted apple trees in large parts of Ohio, Indiana, and Illinois. p. 201

Edison, Thomas (1847–1931) American inventor. He invented the lightbulb and many other things. p. 254

Estefan, Gloria (1957–) Latin-American singer and songwriter. She shares her Cuban culture through her music. p. 257

George III of England (1738–1820) English King. He was against the colonists' fight for independence. p. 186

Gutenberg, Johannes (c. 1400–1468) German metalworker and inventor. He invented the printing press and movable type. p. 144

Henry, John African American railroad worker in American legends. He is said to have raced against a steam hammer and won. p. 201

Jefferson, Thomas (1743–1862) The third President of the United States. He helped write the Declaration of Independence. p. 190

King, Dr. Martin Luther, Jr. (1929–1968) African American civil rights leader. He received the Nobel Peace Prize for working to change unfair laws. p. 208

Lincoln, Abraham (1809–1865) The 16th President of the United States. He was President during the Civil War. He helped make it against the law to own slaves. p. 199

Montañez, Wanda (1964–) American businesswoman. Her clothing designs honor her Hispanic heritage. p. 282

Oakley, Annie (1860–1926) American entertainer. She was very skilled in shooting and showed that women could do many things. p. 287

Parks, Rosa (1913–2005) African American civil rights leader. She refused to give up her seat on a bus to a white man. p. 215

Pei, Ieoh Ming (1917–) Asian American architect. He designs interesting buildings, such as the John F. Kennedy Presidential Library in Boston, Massachusetts. p. 256

Pitcher, Molly (1744–1832) Hero of the American Revolution. She carried water to the soldiers during the war. p. 188

Revere, Paul (1735–1818) Hero of the American Revolution. He warned the colonists in Massachusetts that the British soldiers were coming. p. 190

Roosevelt, Franklin D. (1882–1945) The 32nd President of the United States. He was President during World War II and worked for world peace. p. 35

Ross, Betsy (1752–1836) American seamstress. In American legends, she sewed the first American flag. p. 201

Salem, Peter (1750–1816) African American soldier. He fought in the Battle of Bunker Hill against the British. p. 188

Tan, Amy (1952–) Asian American writer. Her stories about the Chinese culture are read all over the world. p. 244

Truth, Sojourner (1797–1883) African American slave. She helped end slavery and worked for women's right to vote. p. 200

Tubman, Harriett (1820–1913) African American slave. She helped guide slaves to freedom on the Underground Railroad. p. 200

Tutankhamen (c. 1343–1323 B.C.) Egyptian Pharaoh. He became the Pharaoh when he was ten years old. p. 27

Washington, George (1732–1799) First President of the United States. He is known as "The Father of Our Country." p. 191

Picture Glossary

The Picture Glossary has important words and their definitions. They are listed in alphabetical (ABC) order. The pictures help you understand the meanings of the words. The page number at the end tells where the word is first used.

absolute location

The exact location of a place. The **absolute location** of the post office is 394 Oak Street. (page 67)

bank

A business that looks after people's money. People put money in the **bank** to keep it safe. (page 290)

ballot

A list of all the choices for voting. The voter marked her choice on the **ballot**. (page 28)

bar graph

A graph that uses bars to show how many or how much. This **bar graph** shows the money saved each month. (page 280)

barter

To exchange something without using money. People can **barter** instead of using money. (page 308)

business

The making or selling of goods or services. My parents have their own **business** selling flowers. (page 278)

border

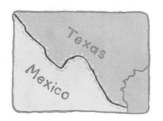

A line on a map that shows where a state or country ends. The red line shows the **border** between Texas and Mexico. (page 46)

calendar

A chart that keeps track of the days in a week, month, or year. A **calendar** shows that there are seven days in a week. (page 250)

budget

A plan that shows how much money you have and how much money you spend. I make a **budget** every month. (page 290)

capital

A city in which a state's or country's government meets and works. Washington, D.C., is the **capital** of the United States. (page 33)

capital resources

All of the tools used to produce goods and services. A factory machine is a **capital resource**. (page 297)

citizen

A person who lives in and belongs to a community. Nick is a **citizen** of the United States. (page 8)

cardinal directions

The main directions of north, south, east, and west. The **cardinal directions** help you find places on a map. (page 90)

city

A very large town. There are many tall buildings in my **city**. (page 111)

change

What happens when something becomes different. In fall, some leaves **change** color. (page 174)

climate

The kind of weather a place has over a long time. The rain forest has a very wet **climate**. (page 86)

colony

colony
A place that is ruled by another country. Virginia was the first English **colony** in North America. (page 180)

compass rose

compass rose
The symbol on a map that shows directions. The **compass rose** shows directions. (page 94)

communication
The sharing of ideas and information. The firefighter uses a radio for **communication** with other firefighters. (page 140)

conflict
What happens when people have different points of view on what to do or how to do it. There was a **conflict** about the rules of the game. (page 242)

community
A group of people who live or work together. It is also the place where people live. My family has lived in our **community** for many years. (page 8)

Congress
The group of citizens chosen to make decisions for our country. **Congress** votes on new laws. (page 34)

consequence

Something that happens because of what a person does. The **consequence** of wearing muddy shoes is a dirty floor. (page 12)

consumer

A person who buys and uses goods and services. This **consumer** is buying fruit for a snack. (page 279)

conservation

The saving of resources to make them last longer. **Conservation** of electricity is a good idea. (page 118)

continent

One of the seven main land areas on Earth. We live on the **continent** of North America. (page 110)

Constitution

A written set of rules that the government must follow. Our **Constitution** says that every adult citizen has the right to vote. (page 37)

council

A group of citizens chosen to make decisions for all the people. The **council** is discussing where to build the playground. (page 42)

country

An area of land with its own people and laws. We are proud of our **country**, the United States of America. (page 111)

diagram

A picture that shows the parts of something. The **diagram** helped me put my toy together. (page 176)

culture

A group's way of life. Music and dance are parts of my **culture**. (page 226)

diversity

Different ideas and ways of living. Many cultures bring **diversity** to our country. (page 240)

custom

A group's way of doing something. One Hawaiian **custom** is to give flowers to visitors. (page 246)

election

A time when people vote for their leaders. The **election** to choose the President is held in November. (page 25)

PICTURE GLOSSARY

R27

environment

All of the things around us. We need to take care of our **environment**. (page 132)

factory

A building in which people use machines to make goods. Many people work at the **factory**. (page 296)

equator

An imaginary line that divides Earth into northern and southern halves. Most of South America is south of the **equator**. (page 90)

fiction

Stories that may seem real, but in which some of the information is made up. The story of Little Red Riding Hood is **fiction**. (page 206)

F

Neil Armstrong was the first person to walk on the moon.

fact

A piece of information that is true. It is a **fact** that humans have walked on the moon. (page 206)

flowchart

A chart that shows the steps needed to make or do something. The **flowchart** shows how to make a picture frame. (page 300)

freedom

The right of people to make their own choices. Americans have the **freedom** to vote. (page 186)

future

The time yet to come. She studies hard to prepare for the **future**. (page 173)

free enterprise

The freedom to start and run any kind of business. **Free enterprise** helps these children earn money. (page 286)

 G

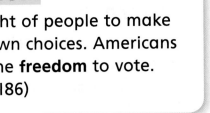

geography

The study of Earth and its people. **Geography** teaches us about Earth and the people on it. (page 18)

fuel

A resource, such as oil, that can be burned for heat or energy. Gasoline is a **fuel** used in cars. (page 117)

globe

A model of Earth. We can find countries on our classroom **globe**. (page 110)

goods

Things that can be bought and sold. This store sells many kinds of **goods**. (page 277)

governor

The leader of a state's government. Every state has a **governor**. (page 26)

government

The group of citizens that runs a community, state, or country. Our **government** needs strong leaders. (page 18)

gulf

A large body of ocean water that is partly surrounded by land. The **Gulf** of Mexico is between Mexico and the United States. (page 80)

government service

A service that a government provides for citizens. Police officers provide a **government service**. (page 20)

 H

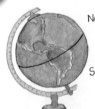

hemisphere

Half of Earth. The northern **hemisphere** is north of the equator. (page 91)

heritage

The traditions and values passed on by the people who lived before us. My grandmother teaches me about my **heritage**. (page 196)

human resources

The work people do to produce goods and services. This worker provides a **human resource** for his company. (page 296)

hero

A person who has done something brave or important. This **hero** saved someone's life. (page 200)

I

immigrant

A person who comes from another place to live in a country. My great-grandfather was an Irish **immigrant**. (page 236)

history

The study of things that happened in the past. The **history** of our country is interesting. (page 178)

income

The money people earn for the work they do. Miguel will use his **income** to buy lemonade. (page 284)

independence

The freedom of people to choose their own government. George Washington fought for **independence**. (page 187)

island

A landform with water all around it. Deep blue water surrounds the **island**. (page 79)

intermediate directions

The directions in between the cardinal directions. Northeast is an **intermediate direction**. (page 94)

J

judge

The leader of a court. The **judge** listened to both sides of the case. (page 19)

L

landform

A kind of land with a special shape, such as a mountain, hill, or plain. A mountain is a large **landform**. (page 76)

invention

A new product that has not been made before. The lightbulb was Thomas Edison's **invention**. (page 254)

landmark

A feature that makes a location special. The Alamo is a Texas **landmark**. (page 197)

legend

A story passed down through history. People in a **legend** do heroic things, but some of these actions are made up. (page 201)

language

The words or signs that people use to communicate. Some people use sign **language** to communicate. (page 227)

legislature

A group of citizens chosen to make decisions for a state. The **legislature** will decide if a new park is needed. (page 43)

law

A rule that people in a community must follow. A speed limit **law** keeps people safe. (page 11)

location

The place where something is. The map will help you find your **location**. (page 66)

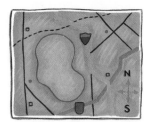

map

A drawing that shows where places are. Can you find a lake on this **map**? (page 110)

map symbol

A small picture or shape on a map that stands for a real thing. This **map symbol** stands for a mountain. (page 113)

map grid

A set of lines that divide a map into columns and rows of squares. The star is at square C-3 on the **map grid**. (page 70)

map title

The title of a map. The **map title** tells what the map shows. (page 113)

map key

The part of a map that shows what the symbols mean. Look for the symbol of the bridge in the **map key**. (page 46)

marketplace

A place where goods and services are bought and sold. This **marketplace** has many stores. (page 304)

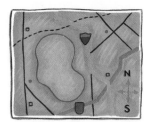

PICTURE GLOSSARY

mayor

mayor

The leader of a city or town government. The **mayor** makes important decisions for our community. (page 26)

memorial

memorial

Something people create to remember a person or an event. This **memorial** reminds us of a brave American. (page 198)

 N

natural resource

Something found in nature that people can use. Oil is a **natural resource**. (page 114)

nonfiction

nonfiction

Stories that contain only facts. Newspaper stories are **nonfiction**. (page 206)

 O

occupation

The work a person does to earn money. My dad's **occupation** is being a doctor. (page 284)

ocean

ocean

A very large body of salty water. Ships sail across the **ocean**. (page 110)

past

The time before now. In the **past**, people used horses for transportation. (page 172)

pole

A point on Earth farthest from the equator. The North **Pole** is the point farthest north on a globe. (page 91)

peninsula

A landform that has water on only three sides. Part of Florida is a **peninsula**. (page 79)

present

The time right now. Today is the **present**. (page 173)

picture graph

A graph that uses pictures to stand for numbers of things. The **picture graph** shows that the most people chose baseball. (page 120)

President

The leader of the United States government. George W. Bush is the 43rd **President** of the United States. (page 26)

problem

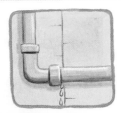

Something that is difficult to solve or hard to understand. The leaking pipe is a **problem** that we must deal with. (page 14)

product map

A map that shows where products are made or found. This **product map** shows where corn is grown in Michigan. (page 136)

producer

A person who grows, makes or sells products. This **producer** grows fruit to sell. (page 276)

raw material

A resource used to make a product. Wood is a **raw material** used to make furniture. (page 295)

product

Something that is made by nature or by people. Applesauce is a **product** made from apples. (page 136)

region

An area of land with the same features. We live in a mountain **region**. (page 82)

relative location

A description of a place that tells what it is near. The **relative location** of my house is next to the park. (page 66)

route

A way to go from one place to another. The **route** shown on this map is easy to follow. (page 142)

responsibility

Something that a person should take care of or do. It is my **responsibility** to take these glasses I found to the store manager. (page 10)

rural

An area in the country, usually far from a city. This **rural** area is very peaceful. (page 126)

 S

right

A freedom. Freedom of speech is one **right** we have as American citizens. (page 9)

scarce

Hard to find because there is not much of it. When money is **scarce**, George cannot buy candy. (page 303)

scientist

A person who observes things and makes discoveries. Albert Einstein was a **scientist**. (page 254)

solution

A way to solve a problem. The **solution** to the leaky pipe problem is to replace the pipe. (page 14)

services

Work done for others. We paid the waiter for his **services**. (page 277)

source

A place something comes from. An encyclopedia is a good **source** of information. (page 184)

settler

One of the first people to make a home in a new place. The **settler** worked hard to farm the land. (page 180)

state

A part of a country. Ohio is one **state** of the fifty states in our country. (page 111)

suburb

A community near a large city. This **suburb** is about ten miles from the city. (page 128)

tax

Money paid to the government and used to pay for services. The **tax** we pay at the store helps pay for building roads. (page 21)

Supreme Court

The court that decides on laws for the United States. The **Supreme Court** hears the most important cases. (page 36)

technology

The use of new objects and ideas in everyday life. Computers are a useful **technology**. (page 134)

Class Rides

	BIKE	SCOOTER
Mike		✔
Jane	✔	
Maya		✔
Eric		✔

table

A chart that shows information in rows and columns. A **table** can be used to compare things. (page 88)

time line

A line that tells when things happened. This **time line** shows holidays. (page 192)

trade

The exchange of one thing for another. Is this a fair **trade**? (page 309)

urban

In, of, or like a city. They live in an **urban** area. (page 128)

tradition

Something that is passed on from older family members to children. Wearing kilts is a Scottish **tradition**. (page 246)

 V

vote

A choice that gets counted. Every person's **vote** is important in an election. (page 28)

transportation

The moving of goods and people from place to place. Buses and airplanes are both used for **transportation**. (page 139)

 W

wants

Things that people would like to have. I have more **wants** than I can afford. (page 288)

Index

The index tells where information about people, places, and events in this book can be found. The entries are listed in alphabetical order. Each entry tells the page or pages where you can find the topic.

For permission to reprint copyrighted material, grateful acknowledgment is made to the following sources:

Alfred Publishing, on behalf of Abilene Music: Lyrics from "What a Wonderful World" by George David Weiss and Bob Thiele. Lyrics copyright © 1967 by Range Road Music Inc., Quartet Music Inc., and Abilene Music, Inc. Lyrics copyright renewed and assigned to Range Road Music Inc., Quartet Music Inc., and Abilene Music. International copyright secured.

Atheneum Books for Young Readers, an imprint of Simon & Schuster Children's Publishing Division: Illustrations by Ashley Bryan from *What a Wonderful World* by George David Weiss and Bob Thiele. Illustrations copyright © 1995 by Ashley Bryan.

Candlewick Press, Inc.: Cowver illustration by Peter H. Reynolds from *Judy Moody Declares Independence* by Megan McDonald. Illustration copyright © 2005 by Peter H. Reynolds.

Capstone Press: Cover photograph from *From Corn to Cereal* by Roberta Basel. Photograph © 2003 by Capstone Press.

Clarion Books/Houghton Mifflin Company: Cover illustration by Giulio Maestro from *The Story of Money* by Betsy Maestro. Ilustration copyright © 1993 by Giulio Maestro.

Dorling Kindersley Limited, London: From *The Random House Children's Encyclopedia.* Text copyright © 1991 by Dorling Kindersley Ltd. Originally published under the title *The Dorling Kindersley Children's Illustrated Encyclopedia,* 1991.

Dutton Children's Books, A Division of Penguin Young Readers Group, A Member of Penguin Group (USA) Inc., 345 Hudson St., New York, NY 10014: Cover illustration by Jennie Maizels from *The Amazing Pop-Up Geography Book* by Kate Petty. Illustration copyright © 2000 by Jennie Maizels.

Phyllis Fogelman Books, A Division of Penguin Young Readers Group, A Member of Penguin Group (USA) Inc., 345 Hudson St., New York, NY 10014: Cover illustration by Karin Littlewood from *The Color of Home* by Mary Hoffman. Illustration copyright © 2002 by Karin Littlewood.

Harcourt, Inc.: *The Tortilla Factory* by Gary Paulsen, illustrated by Ruth Wright Paulsen. Text copyright © 1995 by Gary Paulsen; illustrations copyright © 1995 by Ruth Wright Paulsen.

Heinemann Library, a division of Reed Elsevier Inc., Chicago, Illinois: From *Lives and Times: Harriet Tubman* by Emma Lynch. Copyright © 2005 by Heinemann Library.

Holiday House, Inc.: From *Supermarket* by Kathleen Krull, illustrated by Melanie Hope Greenberg. Text copyright © 2001 by Kathleen Krull; illustrations copyright © by 2001 by Melanie Hope Greenberg. Cover illustration from *The Great Trash Bash* by Loreen Leedy. Illustration copyright © 1991 by Loreen Leedy. Cover illustration from *Betsy Ross* by Alexandra Wallner. Illustration copyright © 1994 by Alexandra Wallner.

Henry Holt and Company, LLC: Cover illustration from *Anansi the Spider* by Gerald McDermott. Illustration copyright © 1972 by Landmark Production, Incorporated.

Houghton Mifflin Company: Cover illustration by Lois and Louis Darling from *Silent Spring* by Rachel Carson. Illustration copyright © 1962 by Lois and Louis Darling.

Ideals Children's Books, www.idealspublications. com: Cover illustration by Robert Quackenbush from *The Whole World in Your Hands* by Melvin and Gilda Berger. Illustration copyright © 1993 by Robert Quackenbush. Discovery Readers ™ Series, Ideals Children's Books.

Barbara S. Kouts, on behalf of Joseph Bruchac: "How the Prairie Became Ocean" from *Four Ancestors: Stories, Songs, and Poems from Native North America* by Joseph Bruchac. Text copyright © 1996 by Joseph Bruchac.

Lee & Low Books, Inc., New York, NY 10016: Cover illustration by Michelle Chang from *Goldfish and Chrysanthemums* by Andrea Cheng. Illustration copyright © 2003 by Michelle Chang.

Hal Leonard Corporation, on behalf of Quartet Music Inc.: Lyrics from "What a Wonderful World" by George David Weiss and Bob Thiele. Lyrics copyright © 1967 by Range Road Music Inc., Quartet Music Inc., and Abilene Music, Inc. Lyrics copyright renewed and assigned to Range Road Music Inc., Quartet Music Inc., and Abilene Music. International copyright secured.

Oxford University Press: From *Oxford First Dictionary,* compiled by Evelyn Goldsmith, illustrated by Julie Park. Copyright © 1993, 1997, 2002 by Oxford University Press. US edition published by Barnes and Noble, Inc.

Puffin Books, A Division of Penguin Young Readers Group, A Member of Penguin Group (USA) Inc., 345 Hudson St., New York, NY 10014: Cover illustration by Wade Zahares from *Delivery* by Anastasia Suen. Illustration copyright © 1999 by Wade Zahares.

Random House Children's Books, a division of Random House, Inc.: Cover illustration from *The Cat in the Hat* by Dr. Seuss. TM & copyright © 1957, renewed 1985 by Dr. Seuss Enterprises, L.P.

Range Road Music Inc: Lyrics from "What a Wonderful World" by George David Weiss and Bob Thiele. Lyrics copyright © 1967 by Range Road Music Inc., Quartet Music Inc., and Abilene Music, Inc. Lyrics copyright renewed and assigned to Range Road Music Inc., Quartet Music Inc., and Abilene Music. International copyright secured.

Reader's Digest Children's Books: Cover illustration by David Wenzel from *Way To Go!: Finding Your Way with a Compass* by Sharon Sharth. Illustration copyright © 2000 by Reader's Digest Children's Publishing, Inc.

Salish Kootenai College Press: Cover illustration by Debbie Joseph Finely from *How Marten Got His Spots and other Kootenai Indian Stories* by Kootenai Culture Committee, Confederated Salish and Kootenai Tribes. Copyright © 1978 and 1981 by Kootenai Culture Committee, Confederated Salish and Kootenai Tribes.

Scholastic Inc.: From *Paul Bunyan and his Blue Ox* by Patsy Jensen, illustrated by Jean Pidgeon. Copyright © 1994 by Troll Associates. Cover illustration by Bert Dodson from *If You Were At ...The First Thanksgiving* by Anne Kamma. Illustration copyright © 2001 by Scholastic Inc.

Sleeping Bear Press ™: Cover illustration by Victor Juhasz from *D is for Democracy: A Citizen's Alphabet* by Elissa Grodin. Illustration copyright © 2004 by Victor Juhasz.

The Watts Publishing Group Limited, 338 Euston Road, London, NW13BH: *When I Was Young* by James Dunbar, illustrated by Martin Remphry. Text copyright © 1998 by James Dunbar; illustrations copyright © 1998 by Martin Remphry. Originally published in the UK by Franklin Watts, a division of The Watts Publishing Group Limited.

PHOTO CREDITS

PLACEMENT KEY: (t) top; (b) bottom; (l) left; (r) right; (c) center; (bg) background; (fg) foreground; (i) inset.

COVER
FRONT: (bl) Larry Luxner; (br) Joseph Sohm/ Visions of America; (c) Getty Images; (bg) Photodisc.
BACK: (tl) William Duffy; (t-bg) Photodisc; (b) Getty Images.

ENDSHEETS IMAGERY
FRONT: (bl) Joseph Sohm/Visions of America; Statue: William F. Duffy.
BACK: (bl) Larry Luxner; (bg) Getty Images.

TITLE PAGE: (c) William F. Duffy; (bg) Joseph Sohm/Visions of America.

FRONTMATTER: I2 (b) Bettmann/Corbis; I2 (t) C.E. Watkins/Corbis; I3 (b) Jim Richardson/ Corbis; I8 (t) Getty Images; I8 (b) Zandria Muench Beraldo/Corbis; I9 (c) Getty Images; I9 (t) Greg Cranna/Index Stock Imagery; I9 (b) Greg Probst/Corbis; I12 Richard Hamilton Smith Photography.

UNIT 1:
IN1A (bg) Photri; IN1B (t) Teresa Baker; IN1B (b) Fort Wayne News Sentinel; 1 (t) Taxi/Getty Images; 2 (br) Danny Johnston/AP Images; 2 (t) Lawrence Migdale; 3 (c) Bob Daemmrich/ PhotoEdit; 3 (t) K. Hackenberg/Zefa/Corbis; 3 (b) Reuters/Corbis; 4 Ed Kashi/Corbis; 8 (b) Medioimages/Getty Images; 9 (tr) Jeffrey Greenberg/Photo Researchers; 10 (c) S. Meltzer/ PhotoLink, Photodisc Green/Getty Images; 10 (l) Joe Sohm/Visions of America/PictureQuest; 11 (c) Chip East/Corbis; 11 (br) David Hiller/Getty Images; 12 Ashley Cooper/Corbis; 16 (c) Digital Vision/Getty Images; 16 (r) Thinkstock/Getty Images; 17 (tl) Comstock Images/Getty Images; 17 (tc) Comstock Images/Getty Images; 17 (tr) Digital Vision/Getty Images; 17 (b) Western History Collections, University of Oklahoma Library; 18 (b) Wayne Dominick/Franklin County Public School; 19 (t) Chuck Liddy/AP Images; 20 (t) George Hall/Corbis; 20 (b) Spencer Grant/PhotoEdit; 21 (tr) Siede Preis/Getty Images; 24 (bg) Paula Bronstein/Getty Images;